nickelodeon™

降去神通

AVATAR

THE LAST AIRBENDER™

Created by

Bryan Konietzko

Michael Dante DiMartino

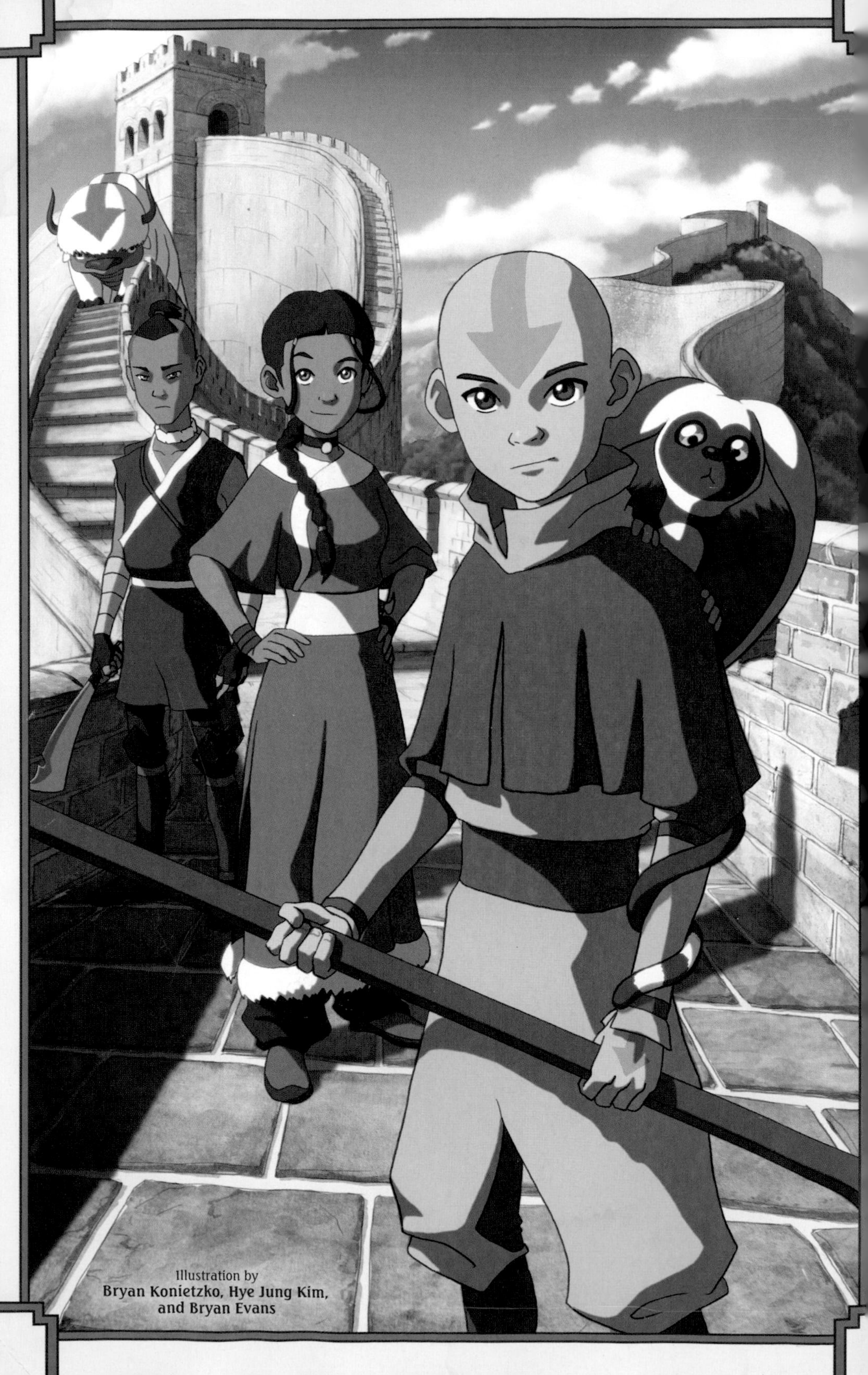
Illustration by
Bryan Konietzko, Hye Jung Kim,
and Bryan Evans

nickelodeon™

降世神通

AVATAR

THE LAST AIRBENDER™

THE LOST ADVENTURES

Featuring

Aaron Ehasz, Alison Wilgus,
Amy Kim Ganter, Brian Ralph,
Corey Lewis, Dave Roman,
Elsa Garagarza, Ethan Spaulding,
Frank Pittarese, Gurihiru, J. Torres,
Joaquim Dos Santos, Johane Matte,
John O'Bryan, Joshua Hamilton,
Justin Ridge, Katie Mattila,
May Chan, Rawles Lumumba,
Reagan Lodge, Tim Hedrick,
Tom McWeeney

DARK HORSE BOOKS

Publisher
Mike Richardson

Collection Editor
Samantha Robertson

Assistant Editor
Daniel Chabon

Series Editors for Nickelodeon
Andrew Brisman, Chris Duffy, and **Dave Roman**

Collection Designer
Stephen Reichert

Digital Production
Ryan Hill and **Susan Tardif**

Cover Illustration
Bryan Konietzko

Special thanks to Linda Lee, Kat VanDam, James Salerno, and Brian Smith at Nickelodeon, to Dave Roman, and to Bryan Konietzko and Michael Dante DiMartino.

This volume collects previously unpublished comics, the *Avatar: The Last Airbender* seasons two and three exclusive DVD minicomics, the *Avatar: The Last Airbender Free Comic Book Day 2011* comic, and comics originally published in *Nickelodeon Comics* #31, #33, and #35, *Nickelodeon Magazine* #124, #127, #133, #140, and #158, and *Nick Mag Presents* #18 and #23.

Published by Dark Horse Books
A division of Dark Horse Comics LLC
10956 SE Main Street
Milwaukie, OR 97222

DarkHorse.com | Nick.com

To find a comics shop in your area, visit comicshoplocator.com

First edition: July 2011
ISBN 978-1-59582-748-7

15 17 19 20 18 16

Printed in China

Water. Earth. Fire. Air. Only the Avatar can master all four elements, and stop the ruthless Fire Nation from conquering the world. But when the world needed him most, he disappeared. And he's been gone for a hundred years, until now . . .

A young Waterbender named Katara and her brother Sokka rescue a strange twelve-year-old boy named Aang, who's been trapped inside an iceberg at the South Pole. Not only is Aang an Airbender—a race of people no one has seen in a century—he's also the long-lost Avatar! Now Katara and Sokka must help Aang master all four elements so he can face his destiny, and save the world!

CONTENTS

Our first twenty-six stories take place during the *Avatar: The Last Airbender* animated series, and show you what Aang and the gang were up to between your favorite episodes. Our last two stories are special bonus adventures that take place further off the beaten path . . .

BOOK ONE: WATER

BOOK TWO: EARTH

BOOK THREE: FIRE

BONUS STORIES

Three very unique benders created by the winners of *Nickelodeon Magazine*'s Avatar Character Contest try out for a spot on Team Avatar!

A hilarious story in the spirit of the "super deformed" (or "SD") shorts that were created for the book two DVD box set!

Book One
WATER

BEE CALM

Story by Joshua Hamilton and John O'Bryan, art by Justin Ridge, colors by Hye Jung Kim, and lettering by Clem Robins.

I THINK I BOTHERED THEM!
SWOOOOOSH
YOU THINK?!

GO TO THAT SMOKE! SMOKE MAKES BEES TIRED!
GOOD IDEA!

FOOOSH

WHEW! THAT WAS A CLOSE ONE.

DON'T MOVE!

DON'T BOTHER IT AND IT WON'T BOTHER YOU.
THE END

Story by Tim Hedrick, art by Justin Ridge, colors by Hye Jung Kim, and lettering by Comicraft.

AAAAAAAH!

SLAM!
SPLAT!

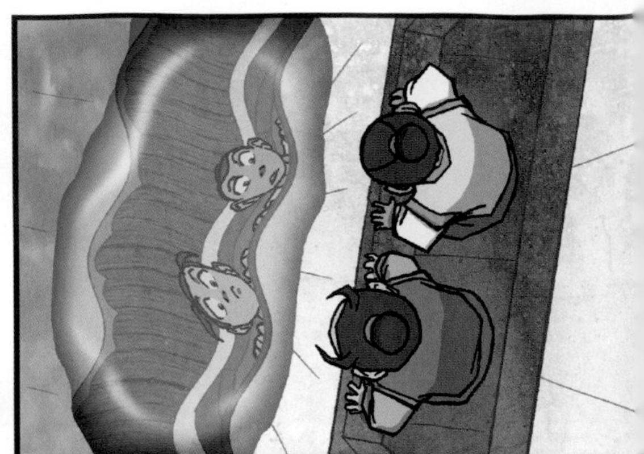

SPLASH!

HOORAY!
HA HA HA HA

ONLY A MORON CHALLENGES A WATERBENDER TO A WATER WAR...
THE END

Story by Alison Wilgus, art by Elsa Garagarza, colors by Wes Dzioba, and lettering by Comicraft.

KEEP YOUR EYES PEELED, GUYS. WHO KNOWS HOW MANY FIRE NATION SCOUTS MIGHT HAVE CAUGHT UP WITH US BY NOW.
AHH... AHH...

YOU KNOW, IN THE WATER TRIBE, WE HAVE WAYS OF TREATING COLDS LIKE THIS.
KATARA, I'M *FINE!* REALLY! I JUST--

ACHOOOOOO!

SNIFF
MRR?

MREEEEEP!
ACHOOOOO!
SPROING
THAT ROPE WAS A GOOD IDEA.
THANKS.

WHEN I WAS A LITTLE GIRL, MY MOM MADE A PASTE OF BLUBBER AND PEPPER BERRIES AND RUBBED IT ON MY CHEST. IT'S A LITTLE GROSS...
A LOT GROSS.
...BUT IT HELPED!
UGH. I'M WITH SOKKA.

THE MONKS USED TO LET THESE THINGS BLOW THEMSELVES OUT, AND THAT'S ALWAYS WORKED FOR ME. I THINK I'LL PASS ON THE BLUBBER-BERRY PASTE FOR...
SNIFF

...FOR...
ACHOOOOO
FWOOOSH
ACK!

WAIT! OVER THERE!
YIKES!
FWISH

TIME TO GO!
WHAT? WHY?
THERE! IT'S THE AVATAR!
SURROUND THEM! QUICKLY!
YEEP!
RRRRRGH!
WOOOSH
MAN, THAT WAS CLOSE! I WONDER HOW THEY FOUND...
...US?
IT'S LIKE GRAN GRAN ALWAYS USED TO SAY: "FEED A FEVER, SLIME A COLD!"
I DON'T THINK THAT'S QUITE IT.
LUCKY FOR ME, I NEVER GET--
ACHOOOOOO!
PASS THE SLIME...
THE END!

Story by Johane Matte and Joshua Hamilton, art by Johane Matte, colors by Hye Jung Kim, and lettering by Comicraft.

HE CAME FROM THE HIGH MOUNTAIN. PROBABLY A TRAVELER WHO GOT LOST.
NO ONE FROM THE NEARBY VILLAGES WOULD GO THERE. THE MOUNTAIN IS SACRED, FULL OF FLYING SPIRITS.

THIS *IS* MORE USEFUL THAN THE STUFF AANG IS LOOKING AT!
AANG, ARE YOU DONE? WE NEED TO GO!
THE MOUNTAINS...

YOU SURE ARE IN A HURRY TO FIND OTHER WATERBENDERS. RELAX, WE'RE ALMOST AT THE NORTH POLE.
IT'S NOT FOR ME! AANG NEEDS A TEACHER AND WE HAVE WEEKS OF TRAVELING LEFT.
THE SOONER WE GET THERE, THE SAFER WE'LL BE.

DO YOU NEED A BLANKET?
NO, I'M OKAY.
WELL... GOOD NIGHT!
G'NIGHT.

I'M SORRY, KATARA. I HAVE TO LOOK INTO THIS.
I'LL BE BACK BEFORE YOU NOTICE I'M GONE.

MAYBE I SHOULD HAVE TOLD KATARA WHAT I WANTED TO DO.

BUT WHAT IF SHE HAD SAID NO? SHE'S BEEN SO FOCUSED ON GETTING TO THE NORTH POLE OVER EVERYTHING ELSE THESE DAYS. BESIDES, SHE BELIEVES ALL THE AIRBENDERS ARE GONE.

BUT I HAVEN'T GIVEN UP HOPE. IF THERE'S ONE PLACE THEY COULD HIDE AND LIVE, IT'S THESE MOUNTAINS.

I HAVE TO HURRY AND COVER AS MUCH GROUND AS I CAN BEFORE GOING BACK. MAYBE I CAN CONVINCE THE OTHERS TO STAY A BIT LONGER IF I CAN FIND...

A STUPA!
AIRBENDERS *WERE* HERE!

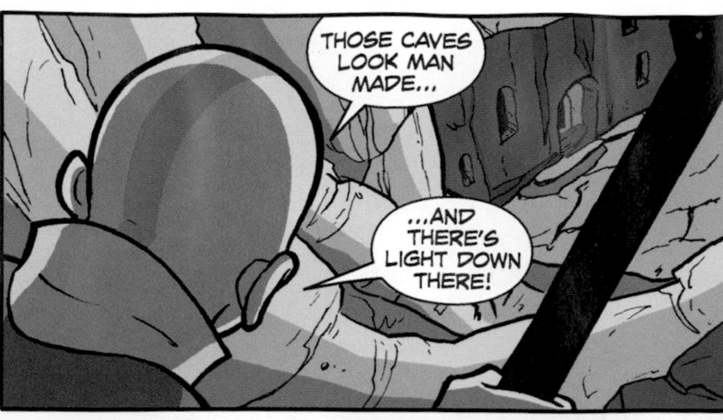
THOSE CAVES LOOK MAN MADE...
...AND THERE'S LIGHT DOWN THERE!

THAT MEANS SOMEONE'S DOWN THERE NOW!

WOW! THIS PLACE IS FULL OF AIRBENDER STUFF!

HELLO?

ERM... EXCUSE ME? ARE YOU...
I MEAN, DO YOU LIVE HERE? DO ALL THESE THINGS BELONG TO YOU?

WHAT!? THE MERCHANT??
NOW! GET HIM!

MAKE SURE HE'S BOUND UP TIGHTLY. WE WOULDN'T WANT HIM ESCAPING AGAIN.
ZHAO. YOU'RE A BIT FAR AWAY FROM THE SEA FOR AN ADMIRAL.

THE SAME TACTIC WAS USED MANY YEARS AGO BY FIRE LORD SOZIN.
THE FEW AIRBENDERS THAT ESCAPED HIS FIRST ASSAULT WERE TOO HARD TO HUNT DOWN. INSTEAD, HE LAID TRAPS FOR THEM.
PLACES LIKE THESE CAVES WERE MADE TO LOOK LIKE THEY WERE INHABITED BY OTHER AIRBENDER REFUGEES.

SOZIN FOOLED THEM USING THEIR OWN EVERYDAY OBJECTS AS BAIT, LURING THEM FAR ENOUGH FOR OUR SOLDIERS TO CLOSE IN.

THIS OLD STRATAGEM STILL WORKS WELL ENOUGH TO CATCH ONE LAST AIRBENDER.

YOUR CURIOSITY AND LACK OF KNOWLEDGE OF OUR MILITARY HISTORY PROVED YOUR DOWNFALL.
"LACK OF KNOWLEDGE."
I BET YOU DON'T KNOW ANYTHING ABOUT AIR NOMADS OR WHAT ANY OF THESE OBJECTS ARE.

MY TURN TO GIVE YOU A QUICK HISTORY LESSON.

IDIOTS! HOLD HIM!!
FOOSH
SNAP
EVER HEARD ONE OF THESE HORNS...
...WHEN AN AIRBENDER PLAYS IT?
BWOOOOOOOOOoooo!

ENOUGH!
I'LL BRING YOUR CHARRED REMAINS TO THE FIRE LORD!
HEY, ZHAO! EVER SEEN ONE OF THESE?
CURIOUS TO FIND OUT WHAT IT CAN DO?
GNAP!
THE DORJE WAS USED IN RITUALS, BUT MY FRIENDS AND I FOUND OUT THAT IF YOU SPUN THEM TOO HARD INSIDE A ROOM, THIS WOULD HAPPEN!
GOTTA GO!
DON'T WORRY, IT WILL SCHTOP BY ITSHELF!
DID YOU KNOW THAT POT ON YOUR HEAD IS A GENUINE AIRBENDER'S C...
SHUT UP.

CAREFUL, KATARA!
IF AANG HAS DISAPPEARED, THAT COULD MEAN WE'RE SURROUNDED BY FIRE NATION FORCES! WELL-HIDDEN FIRE NATION SOLDIERS, WAITING TO AMBUSH US WHEN OUR BACKS ARE TURNED AND...
THERE HE IS!

AANG?

SEE? HE'S OKAY. YOU WORRY TOO MUCH.
WHAT ARE YOU DOING OUT HERE? WE WERE LOOKING FOR YOU.
WAIT, I THINK I KNOW.

THIS PLACE REMINDS YOU OF HOME, RIGHT? ALL THESE MOUNTAINS...AIRBENDERS WOULD HAVE LOVED TO STAY HERE.
THEY WOULD HAVE BEEN ATTRACTED TO THE PLACE.

YEAH.
A FEW OF THEM PROBABLY WERE.

THE END

MOMO in
FRUIT-STAND FREESTYLE

Story, art, and colors by Brian Ralph.

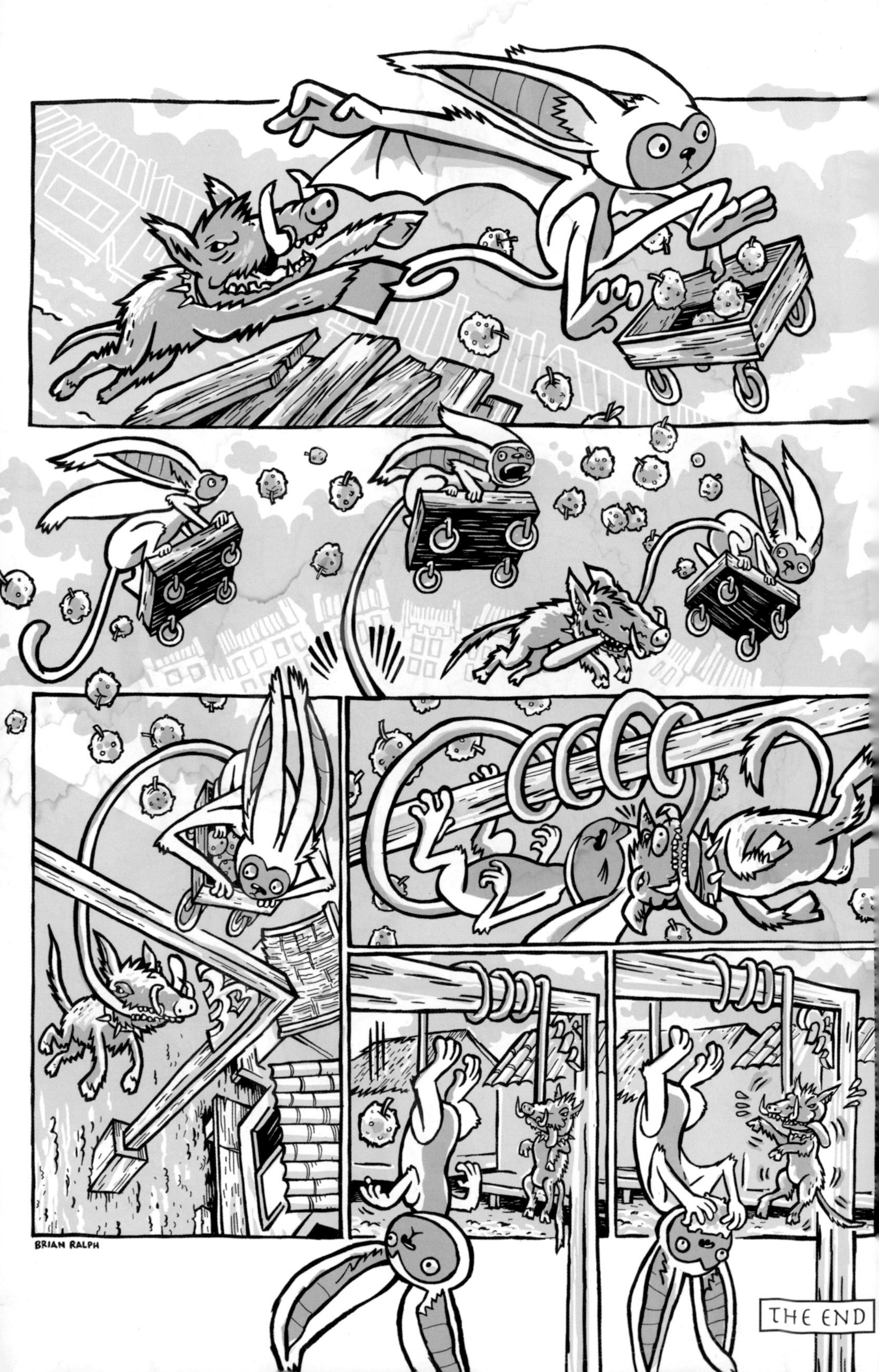
BRIAN RALPH
THE END

Book Two
EARTH

SLEEPBENDING

Story by Joshua Hamilton, art by Joaquim Dos Santos, colors by Hye Jung Kim, and lettering by Clem Robins.

WATERBENDING RODEO!
YEE-HAW...
YOU GUYS READY?
YEP!
LET'S WAKE HIM UP!
WHACK
HEY!
SLIP
NOW!
OOPS.
SLAP
OW!
BOOM
KRAK
KRAK
KRAK
KRAK
KRAK
UH-OH. NOT GOOD.
RUN!
PLINK
WHO, WHAT, HUH?
MORNING, ALL! YOU WON'T BELIEV THE AWESOME DREAM I HAD!
I BET.

THE END

Lessons

Story and art by Johane Matte, colors by Wes Dzioba, and lettering by Comicraft.

CONCENTRATE!
OKAY!
FORGET THE SURROUNDING NOISE. FOCUS ON WHAT'S UNDERNEATH YOU.
STOMP! STOMP! STOMP!

KRIII!
OW! OW!
SHARE! THERE'S PLENTY FOR BOTH OF US!
STOMP! STOMP! STOMP!

GRMPH!
BODOMP
APPA'S GOT THE FRUIT!
GET HIM, MOMO!
BODOMP

KABRAM!

OW!
YOU CAN SHOUT...
...YOU CAN YELL...
...BUT ALL THAT RUNNING AROUND IS DEAFENING!

COME ON, AANG'S LESSON IS FINISHED! LET ME COME DOWN!
NO. YOUR LESSON ISN'T OVER YET.
THE END!

SOKKA THE AVATAR

THIS PLACE SEEMS LIKE THE PERFECT PLACE TO RELAX FOR A WHILE.

AH, FINALLY...I'M SICK OF FLYING. NO OFFENSE, APPA, BUT I'M A *"SOLID GROUND"* TYPE OF GIRL.

EW, ANIMAL PELTS!

GUYS, WE PROBABLY SHOULDN'T STAY HERE TOO LONG... REMEMBER, THE FIRE NATION IS STILL AFTER US.

Story by Joshua Hamilton, art by Justin Ridge, colors by Sno Cone Studios, and lettering by Comicraft.

MY NAME'S SOKKA. I WAS THINKING MAYBE YOU AND YOUR FAKE FOXY FRIEND HERE MIGHT LIKE TO GO OUT WITH ME SOME TIME?
WHAP!

MAYBE THE FOX WOULD LIKE TO GO OUT WITH YOU!
BUT NOT ME!
HEY!
HEE HEE!
THAT'S DELICATE!

YOU KNOW, I'M A REAL HERO. I PRETTY MUCH GO FROM TOWN TO TOWN SAVING PEOPLE AND STUFF.

WELL, THEN, WHY DON'T YOU JUST HURRY ALONG TO ANOTHER TOWN.
BUT MY ADVENTURES ARE INCREDIBLE! HAVEN'T YOU EVER HEARD OF THE AVATAR?!

YOU'RE THE AVATAR?
WELL, ACTUALLY...I, UMM...
YEP, HE'S THE AVATAR!
I AM...? I MEAN, YEP, THAT'S ME.
REALLY? I HEARD THE AVATAR IS THE LAST AIRBENDER. CAN YOU DO ANY AIRBENDING?
OF COURSE I CAN AIRBEND! LIKE I SAID, I'M THE AVATAR...GET READY BECAUSE I AM ABOUT TO MAKE A GIANT HURRICANE!
WINK!
SOKKA... I CAN'T MAKE A HURRICANE...
OH, SORRY...
FORGET THE HURRICANE! WATCH AS I MAKE...
...A SMALL FUNNEL OF WIND!!!

AIRBENDING POWER!
WOW!

MORE AIRBENDING POWER!
=YELP= WHOA!

MAYBE YOU'D LIKE TO GO OUT WITH ME NOW?
OF COURSE! I CAN'T WAIT TO TELL EVERYONE THAT *MY BOYFRIEND* IS THE ***AVATAR!!***

BOYFRIEND?

MEANWHILE, A FEW MILES AWAY, THE ROUGH RHINOS CONSPIRE...
THE AVATAR HAS BEEN SPOTTED HEADING TOWARD A TOWN NOT FAR FROM HERE.
GOOD. WE'LL HAVE HIM IN NO TIME.
OOOH! I LOVE TOWNS!

BACK IN TOWN...
MOM AND DAD, THIS IS MY BOYFRIEND, SOKKA--HE'S THE AVATAR!
YOUR BOYFRIEND'S THE AVATAR?!
I CAN'T BELIEVE THE AVATAR'S ACTUALLY IN MY HOUSE! AND I DIDN'T EVEN CLEAN!
WHO'S THE KID WITH THE WEIRD HAT?

OH, THIS LITTLE GUY? HE'S, UH, MY... SERVANT!

SERVANT...?

BUT SOON...

THERE HE IS! THE AVATAR!

I THOUGHT YOU SAID THEY WOULDN'T TELL ANYONE.

WELL, MAYBE JUST A ***FEW*** PEOPLE.

AVATAR SOKKA, CAN YOU HELP ME?!

ME, TOO! I NEED SOME ADVICE!

HE'S GOT MORE HAIR THAN I EXPECTED.

AANG, WHAT DO I DO?
I DON'T KNOW, SOKKA...
...YOU'RE THE AVATAR. I'M JUST A SERVANT!

MISTER AVATAR! I NEED YOUR WISDOM...
I HAVE AN INGROWN TOENAIL-- COULD YOU HELP ME?
EW!

MAYBE YOU SHOULD WEAR SHOES.
AND WASH YOUR FEET MORE OFTEN!
THANK YOU, MISTER AVATAR! YOU'RE BRILLIANT!
I AM BRILLIANT, AREN'T I?

ALL RIGHT, SINGLE FILE, EVERYBODY. DON'T WORRY. EVERYONE WILL GET THEIR CHANCE TO SPEAK TO ME, THE WISE AVATAR.
I NEED MARRIAGE ADVICE!
ME, TOO!
HEY, AVATAR, I HAVE A QUESTION!

WHERE ARE ALL THESE PEOPLE HEADING?
HAVEN'T YOU HEARD? THE AVATAR'S IN TOWN!
WHAT HAS AANG DONE NOW?
YOU'RE RIGHT... MY HAIR **WOULD** LOOK BETTER CURLY!
THANKS FOR THE ADVICE, SOKKA THE AVATAR.
SOKKA THE AVATAR?
GULP!
KATARA! TOPH!
ARE THESE MORE OF YOUR SERVANTS, SOKKA?
UMM... NOT EXACTLY... MORE LIKE... MY SIDEKICKS!
WHAT?! IF ANYTHING, YOU'RE MY--
HEY!
YANK!

SOKKA, WHY DOES EVERYONE THINK YOU'RE THE AVATAR?
I *KINDA* TOLD THAT CUTE GIRL TO IMPRESS HER. THEN SHE *SORTA* TOLD A FEW OTHER PEOPLE.
RIGHT, JUST A FEW PEOPLE...

YOU GUYS HAVE GOT TO PLAY ALONG... ***PLEASE?***
ONE MORE QUESTION, MISTER AVATAR!

CALM DOWN, EVERYONE, I'LL BE THERE IN A MINUTE.
I WANT TO SEE SOME BENDING!
YEAH, ME, TOO.
WOO-HOO! BENDING!

ALL RIGHT, IF THAT'S WHAT YOU ALL WANT. EVERYONE PLEASE STAND BACK. I AM ABOUT TO DO SOME WATERBENDING.
YOU WANT WATERBENDING? ***I'LL*** GIVE YOU ***WATERBENDING...***

AMAZING!
IT'S ALL IN THE WRISTS...
SWOOSH
CLAP
CLAP

SMACK!
HEY, AVATAR, WHY DON'T YOU EARTHBEND, TOO?!

WOW, LOOK AT HIM GO!
HE'S GOT AN UNUSUAL TECHNIQUE.
BOOMP!

RUMBLE
RUMBLE
I THINK WE FOUND THE AVATAR...

THE ROUGH RHINOS ARE INVADING THE TOWN!
AVATAR SOKKA, SAVE US!
SHOOM!
YOU'RE COMING WITH ME, AVATAR!
SHIINK
GIVE BACK SOKKA!

HE'S OUR PRISONER NOW.
THIS IS NO WAY TO TREAT THE AVATAR.
STAY OUT OF OUR WAY, CHILDREN!
I THINK *YOU'D* BETTER STAY OUT OF *OURS!*
SPLASH!
KEE-- YAAH!
OOH, YOU'VE GOT ME *SHAKING* ALL OVER, BIG GUY.
WHOA!
RUMBLE!

VOOOSH
COUGH!
COUGH!

HMMPH. IS THAT ALL YOU GOT?

I'M NOT IMPRESSED.
ALL OF YOU COMBINED WOULD BE NO MATCH FOR A POWERFUL FIREBENDER--

BOOM!

WHAT HAPPENED? DID I MISS SOMETHING COOL?

WELL, I GUESS NOW EVERYONE KNOWS THAT YOU'RE *NOT* THE AVATAR.
YOU'LL PROBABLY HAVE SOME EXPLAINING TO DO TO A CERTAIN SOMEONE...
I'VE LEARNED MY LESSON--NO MORE PRETENDING.

KISS!

THAT WAS *SO* AMAZING OF YOU! LETTING YOUR SIDEKICKS PRETEND TO BE BENDERS SO THAT THEY COULD SAVE THE DAY FOR ONCE!

MY ONLY QUESTION IS: HOW DID YOU DO ALL THAT BENDING FROM INSIDE THE SACK?
WELL, WHEN YOU'RE AN AMAZING AVATAR LIKE ME, IT'S NOT ALL THAT HARD...

I THINK IT'S TIME WE EXPOSED THAT AVATAR...WHO'S WITH ME?
I'M IN!
YOU KNOW, I ONCE SAVED AN ENTIRE WATER TRIBE.
REALLY?
THE END

DIRTY IS ONLY SKIN DEEP

OH WHERE, OH WHERE HAS MY BADGER-MOLE GONE; OH WHERE, OH WHERE CAN HE BEEEEE?
TOPH! WHY DON'T YOU...JOIN US?
STOMP
STOMP

Story by J. Torres, art and colors by Gurihiru, and lettering by Comicraft.

AND I SUPPOSE YOUR STINK IS MEANT TO REPEL THE ENEMY TOO?

HEH-HEH. IT'S GETTING HOT OUT HERE. WHY DON'T WE ALL JUST COOL OFF?
SPLISH
SPLISH

COME ON, TOPH, I'LL WASH YOUR HAIR FOR YOU...
I DON'T WANT TO TAKE A BATH! LET GO OF MY ARM OR ELSE I'LL...

KRRRUNK
OOF!

OH...SO, YOU WANNA PLAY DIRTY, HUH?

IF YOU WON'T COME TO THE WATER, THEN MAYBE I SHOULD BRING THE WATER TO YOU!
HEY! PUT ME DOWN!
IF YOU SAY SO...
WHOAAA!
SPLASH
KRRSSHHHH
OKAY, THAT WAS KIND OF FUNNY. AND ALSO A BIT MEAN. BUT *MOSTLY* FUNNY.

FAREWELL...FROM MY WATERY GRAVE! TELL THE BADGER-MOLES I SHALL MISS THEM MOST!

SPLAT

GREAT. I JUST WASHED THIS...

LOOK ON THE BRIGHT SIDE. NOW *ALL* OF US ARE COVERED IN A *"PROTECTIVE LAYER OF EARTH"*!

YEAH, LOOK OUT, FIRE NATION...HERE'S MUD IN YOUR EYE!

THE END

DIVIDED WE FALL

I THOUGHT YOU SAID IT WOULD BE SMOOTH SAILING TO HIROKU CANYON!

DO I *LOOK* LIKE A WEATHER ORACLE? THIS STORM CAME OUT OF NOWHERE!

Story by Frank Pittarese, art by Justin Ridge, colors by Hye Jung Kim and Wes Dzioba, and lettering by Comicraft.

SOUNDS LIKE *SOMEBODY* WOKE UP ON THE WRONG SIDE OF THE BISON THIS MORNING.
MAYBE WE SHOULD SET DOWN SOMEWHERE.
THE TREES ARE TOO THICK HERE TO MAKE A SAFE LANDING...
WAIT! THERE'S SOMETHING UP AHEAD!
SOME OF US AREN'T TOO GOOD WITH VISUALS, YOU KNOW. DETAILS, PLEASE!
IT'S A TOWER, TOPH. A MILE AWAY... MAYBE TWO. I THINK WE CAN--

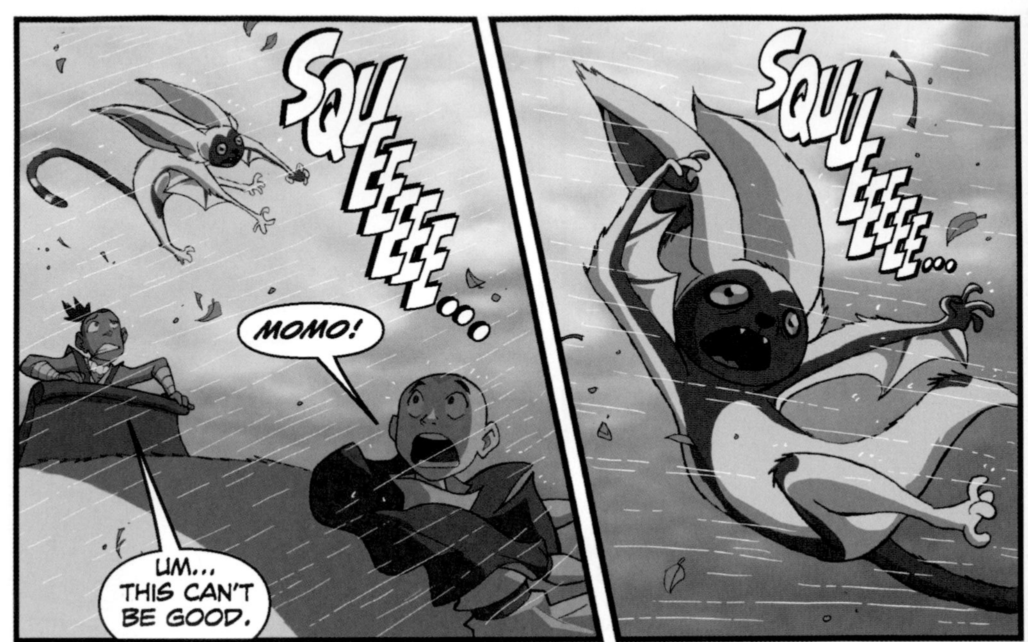
SQUEEEEEE...
MOMO!
UM... THIS CAN'T BE GOOD.
SQUEEEEEE...

...EEEK!
NICE SCREAM, MOMO!

WHEW! THAT WAS CLOSE. GREAT CATCH, TOPH!
AANG!

HI, KATARA!
TURN AROUND!
AAAHH!
HANG ON, I'M COMING!
THIS IS GONNA HURT, ISN'T IT?

MAYBE I CAN...

YES!

SWOOOSH

KATARA!
APPA! MOMO! SOKKA!
ANYBODY!?

GLIDING IN A WIND-STORM? BAD IDEA.

GLIDING WITH TWO HANDS? BETTER IDEA!
AT LEAST THE TREES ARE BLOCKING THE WORST OF THE STORM.

OKAY, SO IF I LANDED HERE, AND WE WERE HEADED NORTHWEST...
...OR MAYBE NORTHEAST...THE OTHERS WOULD BE... ER...UM...

WE AVATARS AREN'T KNOWN FOR OUR SENSE OF DIRECTION.
CHK-KA

MOMO!
SKREE KAAA!
NOT MOMO! *DEFINITELY* NOT MOMO!
SKREE
KAAA!
I'VE GOTTA SHAKE HIM OFF-- *FAST!*

SKEE
GURK!
WHAM

WHEW! YOU SURE ARE A CREEPY LITTLE GUY!

CHK KAAA!
SKIK KAAA!
THIS IS GOING TO BE ONE OF THOSE DAYS.

HAVEN'T YOU GUYS NOTICED...
SKREE KAAA!

...HOW WINDY IT IS TODAY?!?
WHOOSH

THAT WON'T KEEP THEM FOR LONG. BUT IF I CAN HIDE IN THAT CAVE...
SKREE
RIGHT! A CAVE! WHERE VIPER-BATS LIVE!
KRAAA!

BETTER EARTHBEND A CAVE OF MY OWN TILL THESE GUYS PASS!
KRAKK

WELL, AT LEAST THE STORM'S OVER. IF I HEAD FOR THE TOWER, MAYBE I CAN FIND THE OTHERS.
MAYBE.

CHK KAA!

PRRRR KAAAA...

OTHERRSS...

"FIND...OTHERS..."

UM...HEY, GUYS.

YOU'RE, AH... NOT GONNA BELIEVE THIS, BUT WE JUST FELL FROM THE SKY AND--

YEAH, SKINNY BOY. YOU **BOUNCED** OFF MY **HUT!**

WAIT, JUNO. THESE TWO MIGHT BE FUN TO **PLAY** WITH. AFTER ALL, THEY DID DROP IN WITH THESE NIFTY **TOYS.**

DID YOU DROP IN WITH ANY NIFTY **MONEY?**

LOOK, YOU'VE GOT OUR STUFF. GIVE IT BACK AND WE'LL MOVE ON.

YEAH. GIVE IT BACK AND NOBODY GETS HURT.

HOPEFULLY...?

YOWCH! THAT HURTS!
LEAVE HIM ALONE, YOU OVERSIZED ELBOW LEECH!
OOOOH...IS HE GONNA TAKE US DOWN?

HEY! WATCH THE GRABBY HANDS!
YOU WANNA WATCH THE ATTITUDE. COINS, CASH, AND VALUABLES--AND WE CAN ALL LEAVE HAPPY. YOU MIGHT EVEN LEAVE IN ONE PIECE.
SOKKA, YOU BROKE YOUR ARM WHEN WE FELL, BUT HOW ARE YOUR LEGS?
ACTUALLY, I'VE NEVER BEEN CRAZY ABOUT MY KNEES. THEY'RE A LITTLE KNOBBY, AND--

RUN NOW, TALK LATER!
SPLURG!
SPLASH

SHE'S A *BENDER!*

DON'T JUST *STAND* THERE--GET THEM!

WANT SOME FRUIT?

THIS IS GOING WELL.

YOU THINK?

HURRY, YOU DOLTS! WE'VE GOT TO STOP THEM BEFORE THEY REACH...

WASN'T SHARP ENOUGH, ANYHOW...

I...UM... ALREADY HAVE ONE OF THESE.

WATCH THE SEEDS! BITTER!

AREN'T YOU FORGETTING SOMETHING?

ARRRGGH!

FLING

GRAB
USING *THIS* TAKES A *WARRIOR'S* SKILL!
DON'T THINK THIS IS OVER, FREAKS!

I THINK OUR FRIEND HERE NEEDS A COOLDOWN.
I THINK YOU MIGHT BE RIGHT.

YOU HAVEN'T SEEN THE LAST OF-- GLURRGLL!
EWWW! WATER!
WHEEEEE!

I THINK I LIKED IT BETTER WHEN MY ARM WAS BROKEN. LESS TO CARRY. NO CLIMBING.

KILLER THIEVES. YEAH, THOSE WERE GREAT TIMES.

YA KNOW, AANG'S THE AVATAR. HE'S *GOTTA* BE OKAY. APPA'S TOUGH. BUT MOMO...TOPH...

DON'T WORRY, SOKKA. MOMO'S A WILY LITTLE GUY. AND TOPH...?

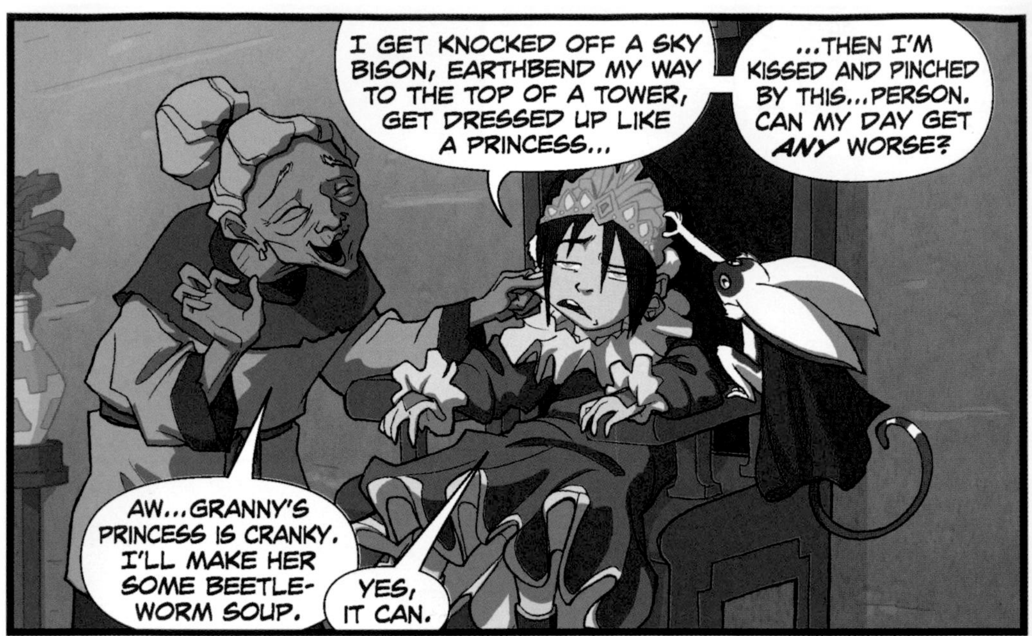
I GET KNOCKED OFF A SKY BISON, EARTHBEND MY WAY TO THE TOP OF A TOWER, GET DRESSED UP LIKE A PRINCESS...
...THEN I'M KISSED AND PINCHED BY THIS...PERSON. CAN MY DAY GET *ANY* WORSE?
AW...GRANNY'S PRINCESS IS CRANKY. I'LL MAKE HER SOME BEETLE-WORM SOUP.
YES, IT CAN.

THE TOWER ISN'T MUCH FURTHER. LOOKS LIKE ANOTHER FEW YARDS...
DO YOU THINK WE'LL FIND FOOD UP THERE? I'M SO HUNGRY. I COULD EAT AN *UNAGI*--OR TWO.

RUMMMBBLLLL
SOKKA, WHAT'S THAT SOUND?
MY STOMACH, NO DOUBT!

SHOOM
THAT IS NOT YOUR STOMACH!
HELLO... OTHERS...!
UM...HI, MR. EARTHBENDER?

LOOK, YOU'RE A *VERY* NICE OLD LADY AND...UM...A *TERRIFIC* COOK.
BUT WE'VE *REALLY* GOT TO FLY. OUR FRIENDS ARE LOST, AND--
HUSH, SWEETIE, AND EAT YOUR SOUP BEFORE THE WORMS CHILL.

CRASHH
LOOK! FOUND... OTHERS!

TOPH! YOU'RE OKAY!
KATARA! SOKKA!

NOT LEAVE EVER! YOU STAY... WITH ME...WITH GRANNY...

NOBODY IS STAYING *ANYWHERE!*

GET AWAY FROM MY *FRIENDS!*

WAY TO OVERREACT, AANG!
OH, MY!
WHOOSH
CRASH!
BASH!
GET... AWAY... FROM... FRIENDS!
AANG...

Grandma Lokai's Earth Orphanage

AANG, STOP!

GRANNY KNOWS YOU'RE NOT HERE TO STAY. BUT IT WOULD'VE BEEN SO LOVELY.
WE'RE SORRY FOR ANY MISUNDERSTANDING, AND WE THANK YOU...
BUT WE HAVE TO MOVE ON. OUR SKY BISON IS LOST, AND--

NO, HE ISN'T. HE'S OUTSIDE, IN THE COURTYARD. BEEN HERE ALL ALONG.
I COULD'VE TOLD YOU THAT, TOO.

FRIENDS... STAY... OVERNIGHT?
WE'D LOVE TO! NOW HOW ABOUT SOME SUPPER FOR A WEARY TRAVELER?

OH, YES!
BEETLE-WORM SOUP FOR EVERYONE! AND IT'S STILL WARM!
GROAN
THE END!

REACH FOR THE TOPH

Story by J. Torres, art and colors by Corey Lewis, and lettering by Comicraft.

TOSS
YOU'LL BE SORRY YOU DID THAT TO AANG!
YIKES.
HWOOOSHHH
KKRRRRSSSHHH
HUH? WHERE'D SHE GO...?

BEHIND YOU, KATARA.
!

NO FAIR! YOU MOVED THE HILL! THAT'S CHEATING!

QUIT YOUR WHINING AND LOOK DOWN NOW.

WHAT... WHAT IS THIS?
QUICKSAND?!
YEAH, AND I COULDN'T HAVE DONE IT WITHOUT YOU.

THE RECIPE FOR QUICKSAND CALLS FOR WATER. SO, THANKS.

WHUP WHUP
WHUP WHUP

ZZZZZZMM
NICE TRY, SOKKA!
I HAVEN'T EVEN BEGUN TO TRY!
UH-HUH.
YOU'RE GOING--
ROLL
--DOWN?
TRIP
I'M WAITING, LOSERS.
OKAY, OKAY...
...YOU WIN...
...YOU'RE THE KING OF THE HILL...
MAKE THAT QUEEN OF THE HILL.
THE END

It's Only Natural

Story by Johane Matte and Joshua Hamilton, art by Johane Matte, colors by Wes Dzioba, and lettering by Comicraft.

IN THE MORNING...
?
SO, BOSCO, ACCORDING TO THIS ENCYCLOPEDIA, BEARS HIBERNATE. I HAVE A FEELING YOU'RE GOING TO BE REALLY GOOD AT THAT--YOU *LOVE* SLEEPING!

WHATCHA DOING?
I'M TEACHING BOSCO HOW TO SURVIVE IN THE WILD LIKE A REAL BEAR.

LET ME SEE THAT.

WHAT... WHAT ARE YOU DOING?
I'M DOING YOU A FAVOR!

THE ONLY ENCYCLOPEDIA YOU NEED IS RIGHT HERE. I WILL TEACH BOSCO HOW TO BE A *REAL BEAR!*
HOW EXCITING!
MRF?

LESSON NUMBER ONE IS THE MOST ESSENTIAL: FINDING FOOD.
BUT *BEE* CAREFUL.
GET IT? *BEE* CAREFUL.
OH, JUST GET UP THERE AND GET IT!
BUT HOW DO WE REACH IT?
WHERE IS NATURE'S LADDER?

COME ON, BOSCO, GET THOSE FANCY CLAWS WORKING.
CLIMB!!!
SIGH

PERHAPS THERE'S ANOTHER SOURCE OF FOOD THAT'S EASIER TO REACH.

FISHING.

NOT LIKE THAT!
A BEAR USES ITS BEAR HANDS.
BEAR HANDS, GET IT?
OH, I'LL SHOW YOU!

JUST LEAP IN...
SPLASH
...GRAB A FISH...
GURGLE... AND... WHOA!
SPLOOSH

EEEEEEEEEEEEEEE
I DON'T KNOW, BOSCO... THIS SEEMS A LITTLE DANGEROUS.
MRF.

SPLISH!
SPLASH!

SPLISH!
SPLASH!
LOOK, BOSCO... NATURE'S FISHING NET!
GROWL!

SHELTER.
FINDING SHELTER IS ALSO VERY IMPORTANT IN ORDER TO SURVIVE IN THE WILD.

AGH! BOARCUPINES!
I SUPPOSE YOU SHOULD ALWAYS MAKE SURE IT'S UNOCCUPIED FIRST.

TERRITORY.
IN ORDER TO DEFEND ONE'S TERRITORY, YOU'VE GOT TO SOUND REALLY FEROCIOUS. SO GIVE ME YOUR MOST FRIGHTENING ROAR.
UM, BOSCO DOESN'T ROAR. BUT HE IS A LOVELY WHISTLER.

SPLENDID WHISTLING, BOSCO.
YEAH, REALLY FRIGHTENING.

SELF-DEFENSE.
IMAGINE I'M A GIANT, ANGRY HOG-MONKEY WHO WANTS TO STEAL ALL YOUR FOOD.
WHAT ARE YOU GOING TO DO?

SBOF!

BOSCO IS WONDERFUL AT PLAYING DEAD.
HE'LL NEVER MAKE IT IN THE WILD.

WELL, THAT WAS A WASTE OF TIME.
ACTUALLY, I THINK I LEARNED SOMETHING TODAY.

THERE ARE SO MANY THINGS I DON'T KNOW ABOUT THE REAL WORLD. HOW COULD I HOPE TO EVER BE A GOOD KING IF ALL MY KNOWLEDGE IS SO LIMITED?

JUST LIKE BOSCO, WHO DOESN'T KNOW HOW TO BE A GOOD BEAR.

IT'S DECIDED! I WILL EXPERIENCE THE WORLD AS A HUMBLE MAN!
MRF!*
*ME, TOO!

THANKS FOR EVERYTHING, SOKKA!
ER... SURE.

HEY, TOPH! DO YOU THINK "KING SOKKA" SOUNDS GOOD?
WHAT? I'M NOT CALLING YOU THAT!
THE END

GOING HOME AGAIN

Story by Aaron Ehasz, May Chan, Katie Mattila, and Alison Wilgus, art by Amy Kim Ganter, colors by Wes Dzioba, and lettering by Comicraft.

THE THRONE ROOM, BA SING SE, CAPITAL OF THE EARTH KINGDOM.

ZU-ZU.

WHAT A PLEASANT SURPRISE.

I'VE FINISHED THE ARRANGEMENTS FOR OUR TRIP BACK TO THE FIRE NATION--WE'LL BE GONE BY TOMORROW NIGHT.

BA SING SE WILL BE SAFE IN HER CARE, AND WE CAN PERSONALLY DELIVER OUR UNCLE, THE TRAITOR, BACK TO THE FIRE NATION.
YOU DON'T NEED ME FOR THAT. I'LL STAY *HERE.*

ZUKO, NOW THAT WE'VE DEFEATED THE AVATAR, FATHER WILL WELCOME YOU AS A HERO. YOU'RE THE FIRE PRINCE AGAIN AND YOU'LL HAVE YOUR OLD LIFE BACK.

I ALREADY SAID, *I'M NOT GOING WITH YOU!*

TY LEE!
STOP WHAT YOU'RE DOING!
AND *LISTEN* TO ME!

MY BROTHER IS BEING DIFFICULT AS USUAL... SO WE NEED SOME EXTRA PERSUASION TO MAKE HIM COME BACK WITH US.

WE KNOW THAT ZUKO AND MAI HAD CHILDHOOD CRUSHES ON EACH OTHER...
...SO, LET'S GET THEM REACQUAINTED.
TOTALLY!

HOW DO WE DO THAT?
AS ALWAYS, JUST FOLLOW MY LEAD. I HAVE A PLAN.

LATER THAT NIGHT...
AZULA, AM I DOING THIS RIGHT?
NO!
WE NEED MORE CANDLES. AND GET RID OF THAT PINK TABLECLOTH! IT HAS TO BE PERFECT.

FASTER! MOVE!!
CLAP! CLAP!
SMACK!
KSH!

WHERE IS EVERYONE? AZULA TOLD ME THAT ADMIRAL LIANG WAS VISITING AND WANTED TO JOIN US FOR DINNER. ALL OF US.
SHE TOLD ME THE SAME THING, MAI. SHE'S UP TO SOMETHING...
WELL, THE FOOD DOESN'T LOOK THAT AWFUL. I GUESS WE SHOULDN'T LET IT GO TO WASTE.

ALMOST TASTES LIKE FIRE NATION FOOD. JUST ISN'T SEASONED ENOUGH.

CAN YOU PLEASE STOP THAT? YOU'RE GIVING ME A HEADACHE!

SORRY. I HAVEN'T PRACTICED IN A WHILE.

TEE HEE HEE!
SNICKER

I KNOW YOU'RE BACK THERE, AZULA! DON'T YOU HAVE SOMETHING MORE IMPORTANT TO DO?

I DON'T KNOW WHAT YOU'RE TALKING ABOUT. I WAS JUST TELLING TY LEE TO STOP MESSING AROUND IN THE BUSHES. IT'S UNDIGNIFIED.
HEY!
DUST

LET'S GET OUT OF HERE.
GOOD IDEA.

UGH... DO PEOPLE ACTUALLY EAT ANY OF THIS?
IT'S NOT SO BAD...ONCE YOU GET USED TO IT.
LEE!? IS THAT YOU...?

LEE, I CAN'T BELIEVE IT! IT'S BEEN SO LONG.
LEE?

WHO'S THIS?
OH...HI, JIN...UM... ER...THIS IS JUST MY FRIEND. MY FRIEND FROM...THE CIRCUS.
YEAH... SHE'S THE KNIFE THROWER.

REALLY?

HERE. I'LL SHOW YOU.
GO STAND OVER THERE, LEE.

HAH! I HOPE SHE'S BETTER AT THROWING KNIVES THAN YOU ARE AT JUGGLING!

HMM... STILL NOT QUITE RIGHT...

BETTER.
FWAPP

CRACK

YOU SEE, IT'S ALL IN THE WRIST, REALLY.

HWIK!

SPLOORCH!
WOW! THAT WAS AMAZING!

YOU WANNA TRY, JIN?
OH!
NO, I COULDN'T POSSIBLY...

...WELL, MAYBE JUST ONE.

HWIK!

KSH!
DODGE

SLP...

KER-SPLOOSH!!
NOW WE'RE EVEN.

SECONDS LATER...
HA HA!
ARE YOU CRAZY!? YOU COULD HAVE GOTTEN ME KILLED!
TK TK
TK
TK
TK

WHATEVER, LEE.
JUST STOP...FOR A SEC!

YOU FINALLY SEEM TO BE ENJOYING YOURSELF.

I'VE MISSED SEEING THIS SIDE OF YOU.
WELL, A LOT HAS CHANGED SINCE THE DAYS WHEN I USED TO THROW MUD IN YOUR FACE.

BUT NOT EVERYTHING'S CHANGED.

LATER...
AWWW, LOOK. THE TWO LOVEBIRDS HAVE GOTTEN BACK TOGETHER.
THEY ARE, LIKE, TOTALLY ADORABLE.

SO...ARE YOU COMING WITH US? WITH ME?
I'D LIKE TO, MAI. I'M JUST NOT SURE I...

POOR, POOR UNCLE...

I WONDER IF HE'LL EVEN SURVIVE THE TRIP HOME.
WELL, WE MUST BE GOING. I SUGGEST YOU BID FAREWELL TO YOUR GIRLFRIEND, LITTLE BROTHER.
NO.

I...I'M COMING WITH YOU.
I'M GOING BACK TO THE FIRE NATION.

DO WHAT YOU WANT, ZU-ZU.
IT'S YOUR DECISION.
THE END

BA SING SE HAS FALLEN.

WE'VE TAKEN SHELTER WITH DAD IN CHAMELEON BAY, BUT TIME IS RUNNING OUT. THE FIRE NATION WILL FIND US EVENTUALLY, AND OUR SHIPS CAN BARELY SAIL, LET ALONE FIGHT.

WITHOUT THE AVATAR, OUR FUTURE IS BLEAK.

THE BRIDGE

AFTER AZULA'S ATTACK, AANG FELL BACK INTO AN UNCONSCIOUS STATE.
IF I'M SUCH A GREAT HEALER, WHY WON'T HE WAKE UP? HOW CAN I EVEN HOPE THINGS WILL CHANGE WHEN I HAVE NO FAITH IN MYSELF?

Story by Joshua Hamilton, Tim Hedrick, Aaron Ehasz, and Frank Pittarese, art and colors by Reagan Lodge, and lettering by Comicraft.

BUT LIFE GOES ON.
FOR A GUY WHO LOST HIS KINGDOM, THE EARTH KING WAS A PRETTY HAPPY GUY... FOR THE SHORT TIME HE WAS WITH US.
GET HIM, BOSCO! HEE HEE!
THE DUKE AND PIPSQUEAK JOINED US AFTER WE CAUGHT THEM TRYING TO STEAL FROM OUR SHIP. THEY'VE BEEN SURPRISINGLY HELPFUL...
...AT LEAST, WHEN THEY'RE NOT GETTING INTO TROUBLE.
WE KNOW WE CAN'T HIDE FOREVER.
BUT, DAD, THE WHOLE POINT OF GOING TO BA SING SE WAS TO GATHER AN ARMY TO INVADE THE FIRE NATION CAPITAL!
YES, SOKKA, I KNOW THAT. BUT THE CITY HAS FALLEN. WITHOUT THE EARTH KINGDOM BEHIND US, I'M AFRAID THAT--
WHAT? WE GIVE UP? THAT'S NOT GONNA HAPPEN!
SPOKEN LIKE A TRUE WARRIOR...

A FIRE NATION SCOUT SHIP WAS APPROACHING. IT WOULDN'T BE LONG BEFORE THEY OUTNUMBERED US FOUR TO ONE.
IF WE WERE GOING TO SURVIVE, WE NEEDED A PLAN--**FAST.**
LISTEN TO ME, HAKODA. IF WE FIGHT THEM, WE'LL BE WIPED OUT. OUR SHIPS CAN'T HANDLE ANOTHER CONFRONTATION WITH THE FIRE NATION!
WE'VE ALSO GOT AANG TO THINK ABOUT.
IF HE'S CAPTURED--OR **WORSE**--THE WHOLE WORLD WILL SUFFER. NO MATTER WHAT, WE HAVE TO PROTECT HIM!
THEN THAT'S WHAT WE'LL DO! ALL WE NEED IS A LITTLE INGENUITY--
YOU'RE NOT GONNA TELL THAT **PENTAPOX** STORY AGAIN, ARE YOU?
AND AN **EXCELLENT** STORY IT IS, TOO, BUT NO.
I WAS JUST GOING TO SUGGEST THAT IF WE CAN'T **BEAT** THE FIRE NATION...LET'S JOIN 'EM!
YOU CAN'T **POSSIBLY** MEAN THAT WE SHOULD SWITCH SIDES?
WE DON'T HAVE TO SWITCH SIDES, JUST **BOATS.**

IT WASN'T SOKKA'S **CRAZIEST** PLAN, BUT IT WAS A **RISKY** ONE. FIRST, WE FLOODED AND SANK OUR OWN SHIPS...
SPLASH
FWOOSHH

BRAMM
KRAK

...THEN, WE **ABANDONED** THEM, LETTING THE FIRE NATION THINK WE'D ALREADY BEEN DEFEATED.

AND NOW, WE WAIT. JUST ONE BIG, HAPPY FAMILY.
BY THIS TIME TOMORROW, WE'LL BE BACK AT **SEA!**
KATARA, IT'S COLD. COME SIT BY THE FIRE...
I'M **FINE.**

THIS IS SOME MESS, HUH? I WONDER WHAT HAPPENED.
WHO CARES! SAVES US THE TROUBLE!

I'LL SEND WORD TO THE FLEET THAT THE WATER TRIBE HAS BEEN DEALT WITH. THEN, WE CAN WAIT FOR FURTHER ORDERS.
SQUAAK
YEAH... AH, YOU GO AHEAD AND DO THAT...

SO, REMEMBER, WHEN THE REST OF THE FLEET GETS HERE, WE LET 'EM KNOW HOW WE WIPED OUT THE WHOLE WATER TRIBE ON OUR OWN.

TOOK US, WHAT, TEN MINUTES? FIVE?
MUNCH
UM, YEAH. AT THE MOST.

THANKS TO GUYS LIKE US, THE WAR WILL BE OVER SOON.
YEP! WE'RE HEROES!
BONK

NEXT CAME THE "EASY" PART-- SNEAKING ABOARD A FIRE NATION SHIP IN THE DEAD OF NIGHT.

I SHOULDN'T BE HERE. I SHOULD'VE STAYED WITH AANG.
RIGHT NOW, WE NEED YOU HERE. AANG WILL BE FINE, AND IF WE PULL THIS OFF, HE'LL HAVE A SAFE PLACE TO RECOVER.

WE EXPECTED A FIGHT. BUT INSTEAD...

THIS IS WHAT WE WERE WORRIED ABOUT? THESE GUYS ARE EASY PICKINGS! WHERE'S MOMO? HE CAN TAKE 'EM!
WHAT'S A "MOMO"?
YOU WERE SAYING...?
WHAT I'M SAYING IS...
...DUCK!
BLLRBRBR
SPLOOSH
GAAAH!
OKAY, SO THE FIGHT TOOK A MINUTE TO GET STARTED...
THWAP
HACK!! HACK!
UGH!
COUGH
FSSHHH
CLANK

COUGH, COUGH
THAT COUGH SMELL! AWFUL COUGH!!
IT'S JUST A LITTLE STINK BOMB. YOU DON'T HAVE TO CRY ABOUT IT!
KRAKK
FWIP FWIP FWIP
WHOA!
KREEKK
SCRUNCH
I STILL CAN'T BELIEVE WE ACTUALLY PULLED IT OFF.
HUH? WHO? WHAT'S GOIN' ON?!?
GOOD MORNING, BIG GUY. YOU'VE JUST BEEN BOATNAPPED!

ONCE WE LEFT THE FLEET BEHIND US, IT WAS TIME FOR A CHANGE OF CLOTHES. LOOKS LIKE FIRE NATION RED IS IN FASHION THIS SEASON.

SOKKA SUGGESTED THAT WE HEAD FOR THE SERPENT'S PASS.
FROM THERE, WE CAN CUT ACROSS THE EARTH KINGDOM AND HEAD WEST FOR THE FIRE NATION.
BUT I DON'T THINK EVIL BARRICADES WERE ON HIS MAP.
YOU'VE GOT TO HAND IT TO THE FIRE NATION. THEY MIGHT BE TYRANTS, BUT THEY CERTAINLY ARE FINE ENGINEERS.

SO WHAT DO YOU PLAN TO DO NOW?

I THINK THERE'S ONLY ONE THING WE CAN DO...
IT'S TIME TO PUT OUR DISGUISE TO THE TEST!

NOW EVERYTHING WAS IN MY FATHER'S HANDS.
WHERE ARE YOU HEADED, SOLDIER?
THE WATER TRIBE NAVY HAS BEEN COMPLETELY DESTROYED. OUR ORDERS ARE TO HEAD WEST TO RENDEZVOUS WITH THE FLEET OUT THERE. SO IF YOU WOULDN'T MIND LETTING US PASS...

GOOD SAILING, SOLDIER!

CRREEEAAAK

BY THE TIME YOU JOIN THE REST OF THE FLEET, THEY'LL PROBABLY SEND YOU STRAIGHT *HOME!*

WHAT MAKES YOU SAY *THAT?*

DIDN'T YOU HEAR? THE WAR'S ALMOST OVER.
THE AVATAR WAS *KILLED* AT BA SING SE!

SO THE AVATAR IS DEAD...

WHAT ARE YOU SO HAPPY ABOUT, SOKKA? THEY THINK THEY'VE WON!

I KNOW.
AND THAT'S JUST THE BREAK WE *NEEDED*.

SOKKA WAS RIGHT--AGAIN. AANG'S "DEATH" WORKS TO OUR ADVANTAGE, AND NOBODY SUSPECTS WE'RE LIVING AS SOLDIERS OF THE FIRE NATION.
AND THAT'S THE BEST COURSE FOR US TO TAKE?
UNLESS YOU'VE GOT ANOTHER SUGGESTION. YOU KNOW, SON, WITH ANY LUCK, WE JUST MAY SURVIVE THIS EXPERIENCE.

HEY, CAN WE STOP AT KIRACHU ISLAND? FIRE NATION FOOD'S STARTING TO GROW ON ME, AND I HEAR THEIR SUPERSPICY SOUFFLÉ IS TO DIE FOR!
PLEASE DON'T SAY THINGS LIKE THAT.

IT'LL TAKE SOME GETTING USED TO--FOR ALL OF US.
SNIFF
UGH. THESE CLOTHES SMELL LIKE ASH.
NOT. FUN.
SQUEE?

BUT IF WE GOT THROUGH THE LAST FEW DAYS, WE CAN GET THROUGH ANYTHING.

WE JUST HAVE TO KEEP ON FIGHTING...
...AND BE CONFIDENT THAT SOON...
...THE AVATAR WILL RETURN.

THE END

Book Three
FIRE

PRIVATE FIRE

Story by Joshua Hamilton, art by Johane Matte, colors by Wes Dzioba, and lettering by Comicraft.

I KNOW!
WE COULD ALL DRESS LIKE REPORTERS AND INTERVIEW THE LOCALS!
REPORTERS?
YEAH, NEVER MIND. THAT PROBABLY WON'T WORK.
LOOK, THE BEST WAY TO GATHER INFORMATION ON *THE ENEMY* IS BY OBSERVING THEM IN THEIR EVERYDAY LIVES.
YOU KNOW--FIND OUT WHAT MAKES THEM TICK.
SOMETIMES I WISH I KNEW WHAT MAKES *SOKKA* TICK.
I DON'T EVEN *WANT* TO KNOW.

SO, WHY ARE WE GOING TO A MARKET?
BECAUSE THIS IS WHERE ***THE ENEMY*** GOES, AND WE HAVE TO FIND OUT ***WHY.***

MY GUESS IS THAT THEY'RE HERE TO SHOP.
MAYBE THAT'S WHAT THEY ***WANT*** YOU TO THINK.

LOOK, A FIRE NATION ***TORTURE CHAMBER!***

ACTUALLY, IT'S JUST A KILN.
LOVELY POTTERY.
YEAH. IT ***IS*** NICE.

SPYING...
HAVE WE CRACKED THE SECRETS OF THE FIRE NATION YET?
I DON'T THINK SO.

...MORE SPYING...
HOW ABOUT NOW?
SHHH...PAY ATTENTION!

...AND EVEN MORE SPYING...
LOOK! WHAT IS THAT STRANGE MAN DOING?
I DON'T KNOW! I CAN'T SEE ANYTHING.
HE'S JUST EATING NOODLES.
THIS IS DUMB.

I HATE TO BE A KILLJOY, BUT I DON'T THINK WE'RE GOING TO LEARN ANYTHING NEW ABOUT THE FIRE NATION BY JUST SPYING ON NORMAL PEOPLE.
?
PFF
SQUEE!
BUT HOW DO WE BREAK IT TO SOKKA? HE SEEMS SO HAPPY WHEN HE'S OBSESSED.
YOU GUYS ARE RIGHT. SURVEILLANCE JUST ISN'T HANDS-ON ENOUGH.
IF WE REALLY WANT TO LEARN ABOUT THE FIRE NATION, WE'VE GOT TO BECOME PART OF THE FIRE NATION.
WHAT ARE YOU TALKING ABOUT, SOKKA?

I'M GOING TO JOIN THE FIRE NATION ARMY!
加入優勝者隊伍*
到附近招募站報名
NOW THAT'S *REALLY* DUMB.
*"JOIN THE WINNING TEAM! SIGN UP AT YOUR LOCAL RECRUIT-MENT CENTER TODAY!"

YOU'RE GOING TO JOIN THE *FIRE NATION ARMY?!*

BOOT CAMP...

WE ARE GOING TO TAKE YOU, BREAK YOU DOWN, AND TURN YOU MAGGOT-SLUGS INTO REAL FIRE NATION SOLDIERS!

PLIC!

EEK!

TODAY, WE ARE GOING TO LEARN TO RIDE A KOMODO RHINO.
PRIVATE WANG FIRE, WHY DON'T YOU BE THE FIRST ONE TO SHOW US HOW IT'S DONE!

ME?

GRAB!

NIIICE KOMODO RHINO...
...PLEASE BE GENTLE.

AHH!
HELP...
...ME!

TODAY IS AN IMPORTANT DAY IN EVERY SOLDIER'S LIFE-- FOR TODAY, YOU WILL GET YOUR FIRE NATION *UNIFORM.*
CAN I GET ONE OF THE HELMETS WITH THE *SCARY SKULL FACES* ON THEM? THOSE ARE WAY COOLER.

MOMENTS LATER...
HEY! I THINK THIS UNIFORM IS TOO BIG ON ME.

MAYBE YOU'RE JUST TOO *SMALL,* PRIVATE FIRE!
BUT I REALLY THINK THAT--
WHOA...

RIP!
OOPS!

YOU JUST EARNED YOURSELF A WORLD OF *PAIN,* PRIVATE WANG FIRE.

COME ON, PRIVATE!
CAN'T YOU MARCH WITH A LITTLE EXTRA WEIGHT?

WE ARE GOING TO BE HERE ALL DAY UNLESS YOU GIVE ME TWENTY PUSHUPS!
JUST TWENTY? NO PROBLEM.

DON'T FORGET ABOUT YOUR FRIEND.
MRUIIK!

I HAVE TO CLEAN ALL OF THESE STALLS?
AND WHEN YOU'RE DONE...

...YOU'LL CLEAN *THOSE* STALLS, TOO!
MRUIIK!

LATER...
DID YOU HEAR THE NEWS?

NEWS?!

IT'S UNBELIEVABLE. THESE GUYS BARELY HAVE ANY TRAINING.
WELL, IT LOOKS LIKE THE DECISION'S ALREADY BEEN MADE...

...ALL NEW RECRUITS WILL BE SHIPPED OFF TO THE FRONTLINE TOMORROW!
GULP

DID YOU HEAR THAT?
WE'RE GOING TO BE *SHIPPED OUT* TOMORROW!
SHAKE SHAKE

GULP
CRUNK!
CRONK!
EEK!
PLEASE DON'T TURN AROUND...PLEASE DON'T TURN AROUND... PLEASE...
PHEW!

WHERE IS PRIVATE WANG FIRE?!
UM... I'M NOT SURE... SIR!
YOU'RE NOT SURE!?
WELL, I EXPECT YOU AND THE REST OF THIS COMPANY TO SEARCH THIS BASE UNTIL YOU ARE SURE!

LATER...
SIR, WE SEARCHED THE ENTIRE BASE. PRIVATE FIRE IS NOT HERE.
?
I ALWAYS KNEW THAT PRIVATE WAS NO GOOD.
NO ONE DESERTS THE FIRE NATION ARMY. NO ONE.
MEN, PRIVATE WANG FIRE IS NOW A CRIMINAL.
GRAB YOUR GEAR, BECAUSE WE ARE GOING TO CAPTURE THAT CRIMINAL AND BRING HIM BACK HERE TO FACE JUSTICE...
...FIRE NATION STYLE!
LET'S MOVE!

NOT MUCH LATER...

HEY, LOOK! SOKKA IS BACK!
SO, HOW WAS ARMY LIVING?
WE HAVE TO GET OUT OF HERE!
I DON'T HAVE TIME TO EXPLAIN...BUT WHEN THE ARMY FINDS OUT I'M GONE, THEY'RE PROBABLY NOT GOING TO BE HAPPY!
AND WHEN THEY'RE NOT HAPPY, THAT'S NOT GOOD!

SO YOU MEAN TO TELL ME THIS WHOLE THING BACKFIRED? LIKE I DIDN'T SEE THAT COMING.
THANKS FOR YOUR SUPPORT, TOPH.
SNIFF?
BY THE WAY...

...YOU SMELL LIKE PIG POOP.
I KNOW! WOULD YOU JUST HURRY UP AND PACK YOUR STUFF!

...OR *NOT!*

FOUND HIM!

YOU'RE IN SOME *SERIOUS TROUBLE* NOW, PRIVATE FIRE!

SO, YOU THOUGHT YOU COULD DESERT THE FIRE NATION ARMY? WELL, YOU THOUGHT **WRONG!**
NO... I...
...I DISCOVERED EARTHBENDER AND WATERBENDER SPIES WHO WERE TRYING TO INFILTRATE THE FIRE NATION! I TRACKED THEM DOWN TO THAT CAVE!
RIGHT. AND MY GRANDMOTHER'S THE FIRE LORD.
IT'S **TRUE!** AND I CAN STOP THEM IF YOU'LL JUST LET ME GO!
I DON'T THINK SO.

UH...THE ARMY'S HERE.
AND THAT ARMY IS TAKING SOKKA AWAY!
JUST FOR THE RECORD, I KNEW SOMETHING LIKE THIS WOULD HAPPEN.
LET'S SHOW THEM THAT SOKKA'S NOT LYING. THERE ARE EARTHBENDERS AND WATERBENDERS HERE!
FWAK
SPLASH
ROAR!
WHOOSH
SKREE!

VOOSH
GASP!
RUMBLE
SPLASH

PRIVATE FIRE WAS TELLING THE TRUTH! WHAT DO WE DO?!

UMM, SIR... WHAT ARE YOUR ORDERS?
GULP!

DRILL SERGEANT, IF YOU DON'T MIND, I'LL TAKE CARE OF THOSE DANGEROUS BENDERS MYSELF.
YES! LET'S DO THAT!

RUMBLE
SPLASH

EARTHBENDERS AND WATERBENDERS, PREPARE TO MEET YOUR DOOM!
THERE GOES ONE BRAVE SOLDIER.

WE'VE GOT TO GET OUT OF HERE! THERE'S A WHOLE ARMY OUT THERE! WHAT DO WE DO?! WHAT DO WE DO??!!!
YEAH, YOU'RE ONE *BRAVE* SOLDIER ALL RIGHT.

CALM DOWN. WE'LL BE FINE!

TOPH, YOU EARTHBEND A HOLE SO WE CAN ESCAPE OUT THE BACK. AANG AND SOKKA, YOU TWO MAKE IT SOUND LIKE THERE'S A FIGHT GOING ON IN HERE.
I'M ON IT!
OKAY!

BOOM
BOOM

EW! UGH! WHACK! TAKE THAT!

UGH! TAKE THAT!
RUMBLE
SPLASH
VOOSH
IT'S CAVING IN!
PRIVATE FIRE, NOOOO!!!

IT'S SO SAD...
HA HA!

NIGHT ANIMALS

Story by Katie Mattila, art by Justin Ridge, colors by Wes Dzioba, and lettering by Comicraft.

ROAAAAAR
SCREEEEECH

AAAAAAAH!

THE NEXT MORNING...
YAWN!
THESE MANGOES ARE GREAT! THANKS, SOKKA.
YEAH! I ALREADY ATE LIKE SIX OF THEM!
ACTUALLY... I DON'T FEEL SO GOOD...

WHEN DID I HAVE TIME TO PICK MANGOES?
LOOK AT YOU TWO! YOU ARE SO LAZY!
YOU KNOW, WE HAVE A BIG DAY AHEAD OF US!
ZZZZZZZZZZ
THE END

Boys' Day Out

THE AVATAR AND HIS FRIENDS ARE MAKING THEIR WAY THROUGH THE FIRE NATION, CAMPING OUT IN DISGUISE.

COME ON, GUYS, WE'VE BEEN STUCK UP HERE FOR DAYS AND THERE'S A ***WHOLE TOWN*** JUST SITTING THERE! CAN'T WE GO OUT AND ***DO*** SOMETHING FOR ONCE?

SHHHHH! CONCENTRATING!!!

SORRY, KATARA, BUT I REALLY NEED TO GET THIS BALANCE RIGHT. MAYBE LATER?

Story by Alison Wilgus, art and colors by Gurihiru, and lettering by Comicraft.

NICE.
VERY NICE.
SLURP
CLANK
WHOOHOO!

I GOTTA HAND IT TO YOU, KATARA. THIS ACTUALLY SEEMS LIKE IT COULD BE FUN.

CAN I HELP YOU?

YES, ACTUALLY! TWO FOR DINNER, PLEASE!

SNORT
I DON'T THINK SO, KID.

BUT...
LET ME HANDLE THIS.
MOVE IT, TINY. THERE'S A STEAK IN THERE WITH MY NAME ON IT.
FIND SOMEWHERE ELSE TO EAT, PRINCESS. THIS AIN'T NO PLACE FOR LITTLE GIRLS.

THE NERVE OF THAT GUY! I COULD KICK HIS BUTT WITH MY PINKIE FINGER, AND HE'S TELLING ME I CAN'T GO IN JUST BECAUSE I'M A GIRL? NOW I'M MAD AND HUNGRY!

COME ON, LET'S GO FIND SOME STUPID, FRILLY TEA SHOP. AT LEAST THEY'LL MAKE ME A SANDWICH.
HOLD ON... IF BEING A GIRL IS WHAT'S KEEPING US FROM GETTING IN...

"...THEN WE'LL JUST HAVE TO FIND A WAY AROUND IT!"
HAVE FUN, BOYS!
IT'S NICE TO SEE KIDS YOUR AGE TAKE AN INTEREST IN FINE DINING.

MAN, YOU'RE *FULL* OF SURPRISES TODAY.
THANKS...
BUT, IF YOU'RE SERIOUS ABOUT BEING TOUGH, YOU GOTTA WORK ON YOUR ATTITUDE. IF YOU WANT JERKS LIKE THAT TO TAKE YOU SERIOUSLY, DON'T LET 'EM PUSH YOU AROUND!

NOW, LET'S FIND A TABLE SO WE CAN--

WHAT'S *THAT?*

WHOA, HOLD UP! I THOUGHT WE WERE HERE FOR *FOOD.*

WE'RE HERE FOR *TOUGH,* AND THAT LOOKS PRETTY TOUGH TO ME!

YEAH, BUT--

CRANK IT UP!

WOOOOOOOOO!

I SHOULDA STUCK WITH THE TOE PICKING.

HEY, KID, I'D USE BOTH HANDS IF I WERE YOU! IT'S EASY TO GET--

--THROWN!
OOF!
BUCK
BAM
WATCH IT, KID!
WHO'RE YOU CALLING A KID, TOOTHPICK?
YOU CALLIN' MY PAL A TOOTHPICK?
YEAH, YOU HEARD ME! YOU BETTER STAY OUTTA MY WAY OR I'LL MOP THE FLOOR WITH YOUR FACE!
I'D LIKE TO SEE YOU TRY, YOU LITTLE RUNT.
POKE
SIGH
WIFF
COUNT YOURSELF LUCKY, BUCKO! I'M LETTING YOU OFF EASY!
I THINK THAT'S PLENTY TOUGH FOR ONE DAY.

SIGH

WHAT HAPPENED TO YOUR NIGHT OUT ON THE TOWN?
AND WHY ARE YOU *DRESSED* LIKE THAT?
LONG STORY.
TELL YOU LATER.

ON SECOND THOUGHT, MAYBE BEING GIRLY ISN'T SO BAD.
TEA SANDWICH?
PLEASE.
END

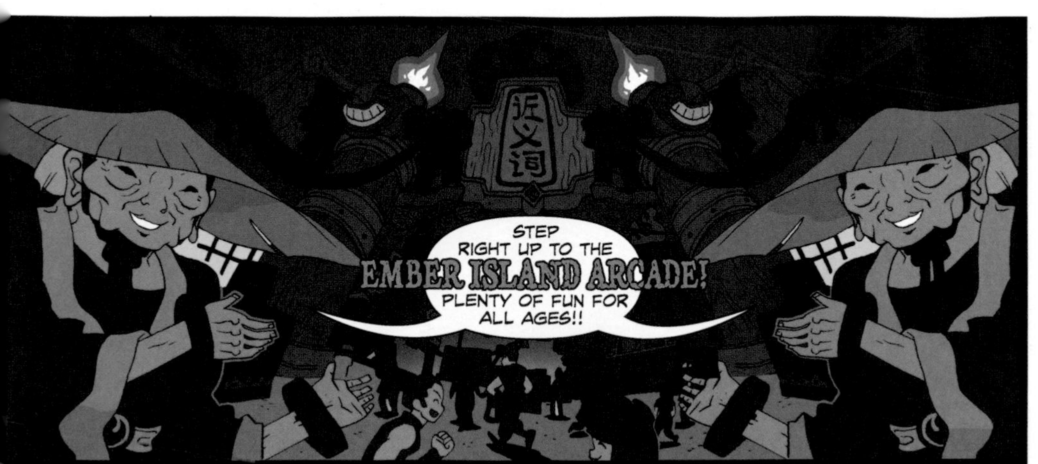

Story, art, and colors by Corey Lewis, and lettering by Comicraft.

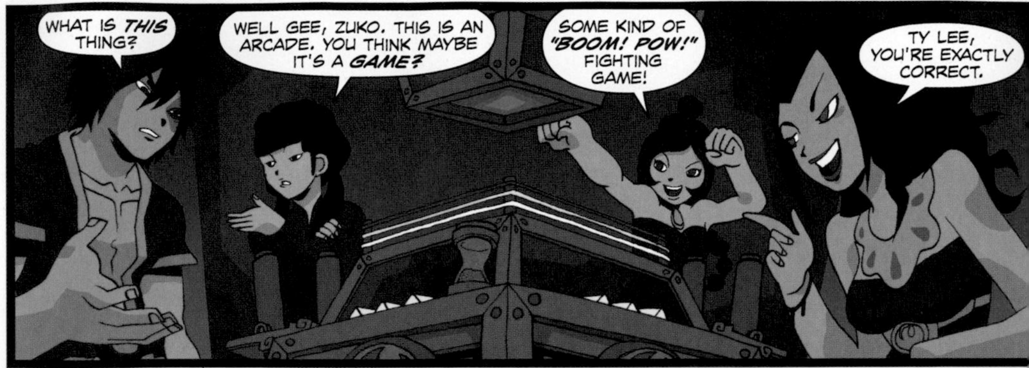
WHAT IS THIS THING?
WELL GEE, ZUKO. THIS IS AN ARCADE. YOU THINK MAYBE IT'S A GAME?
SOME KIND OF "BOOM! POW!" FIGHTING GAME!
TY LEE, YOU'RE EXACTLY CORRECT.

THIS, MY FRIENDS, IS "STREET BENDER," THE MOST STATE-OF-THE-ART IN FIRE NATION ARCADE ENTERTAINMENT.
TWO PLAYERS FACE EACH OTHER USING CUTE LITTLE WARRIOR DOLLS IN THE MOST BRUTAL OF SIMULATED BATTLES...

AZULA, HOW DO YOU KNOW SO MUCH ABOUT THIS THING?
SHE'S BEEN BEATING LITTLE KIDS AT IT ALL WEEKEND.
A PRINCESS HAS TO LAY A FIRM IRON FIST UPON HER SUBJECTS, AFTER ALL.

WHAT DO YOU SAY, LITTLE BROTHER...CARE FOR A MATCH?
NO WAY. THIS IS KID'S STUFF.

OH COME NOW, DEAR BROTHER, DON'T BE SO DROLL. AFTER ALL, THIS IS AN AVATAR-THEMED VERSION OF THE GAME. LOOK! EVEN YOU AND I ARE IN IT.
BUT DON'T WORRY, I'LL SPARE YOU THE HUMILIATION AND REFRAIN FROM PICKING MY OWN CHARACTER.

HERE'S AN OPPONENT MORE YOUR SPEED. OR ARE YOU AFRAID OF FIGHTING THIS LITTLE GUY?

CHALLENGE ACCEPTED!
NOT SO FAST! IT'LL COST YOU ONE SILVER PIECE TO PLAY!

AGH... I KNOW, I KNOW.

CHLING
CHLING
KTHUNK

OKAY!
YOU PICKED YOUR OWN CHARACTER?
YEAH! SO?!

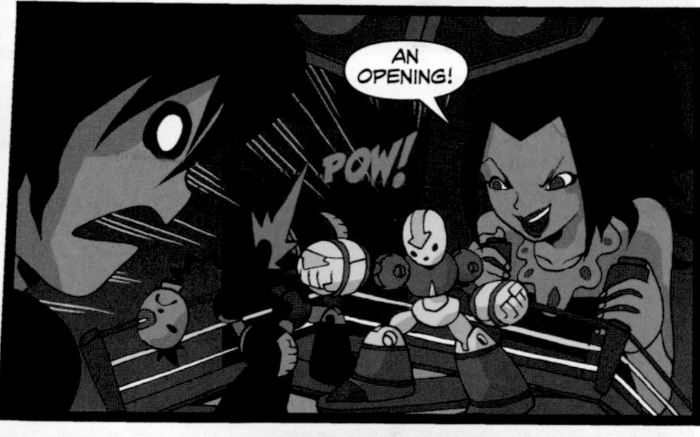
AN OPENING!
POW!

HEY!!! I WASN'T READY!! I DON'T EVEN KNOW HOW TO PLAY!
OH, PLEASE, ZUKO. IT'S NOT THAT COMPLICATED.

RIGHT, LISTEN WELL, LITTLE BROTHER.
THE TWO METAL RODS MOVE YOUR CHARACTER ABOUT THE RING. PRESS THE BUTTONS ON THE RODS TO MAKE YOUR CHARACTER ATTACK.
EACH HIT YOU SCORE ON YOUR OPPONENT COSTS THEM ONE LIFE BAR. THE FIRST PERSON TO DESTROY ALL THREE OF THEIR OPPONENT'S LIFE BARS WINS!

SO THAT MEANS YOU'RE DOWN TO TWO LIFE BARS NOW, ZUKO...
ARGH... THIS IS SO STUPID...

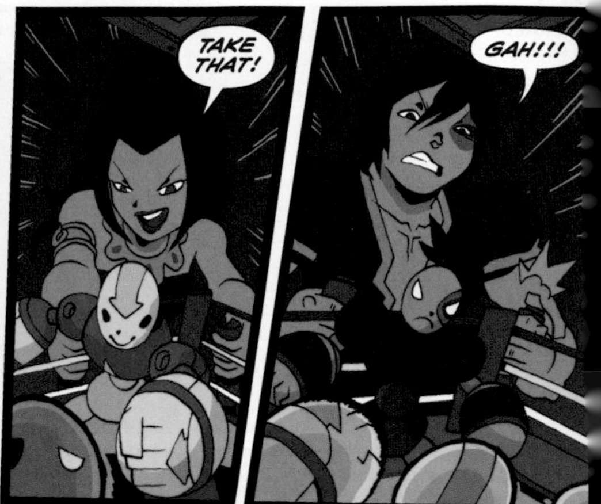
TAKE THAT!
GAH!!!

HA HA!
BAM
HEY! I GOT YOU!!

YES, YES, WELL PLAYED, ZU-ZU... I'LL GIVE YOU THAT ONE.

BUT CAN YOU HANDLE THIS?!

POP!

WHAT WAS THAT!?!
OH, DID I FORGET TO MENTION YOU CAN DO A SUPER ATTACK BY FIREBENDING INTO THE METAL RODS?
YEAH. YOU DID.
SILLY ME.

SO THAT'S THIS GAME'S SECRET...
...HEATING UP THE RODS ACTIVATES SOME KIND OF MECHANISM IN THE FIGURINE THAT SHOOTS OUT A PROJECTILE ATTACK. WELL, IN THAT CASE...

SORRY, BROTHER. ONE MORE HIT AND YOU'RE TOAST.
NOT TODAY, AZULA. TODAY, YOU'RE THE TOAST!! SO GET THE JELLY READY!!!

HUH? WHAT DOES THAT EVEN MEAN?
NEVER MIND! JUST FIGHT!

DON'T MIND IF I DO!
FWAK

NOW'S MY CHANCE!!

HRRAAH!!!

WOW!
OH BOY.
NICE ONE, ZU-ZU.

HMPH. NOW *THAT'S* ENTERTAINING.

AAAH!! MY GAME!! WHO DID THIS?!
ZUKO, YOU REALLY ARE A SORE LOSER.
STUPID GAME DESERVED IT.
WOW, THEY SHOULD REALLY PUT A WARNING ON THAT GAME!!
YEAH, "NO ZUKOS ALLOWED."
END!
COREYYY LEWIS ©2009

MONSTER SLAYER
WHILE HIDING OUT IN THE FIRE NATION...
EARTHQUAKE! EVERY MAN FOR HIMSELF!
NOT EVEN, SOKKA. THAT WAS JUST...
...APPA'S STOMACH GRUMBLING!
IT'S OKAY, BOY. WE'LL HEAD TO THAT VILLAGE NEARBY TO GET SOME FOOD FOR ALL OF US.
YOU WAIT HERE WITH MOMO. DON'T WANT YOUR STOMACH FREAKING ANYONE ELSE OUT.
FOR YOUR INFORMATION, I WASN'T FREAKING OUT! I WAS JUST CONCERNED ABOUT YOU PEOPLE!

Story by J. Torres, art and colors by Gurihiru, and lettering by Comicraft.

SHORTLY, IN SAID PEACEFUL VILLAGE...

SO, WHO HAS MONEY?

UH, YEAH...THAT ***COULD*** BE A PROBLEM.

WELL, I HAVE A COUPLE OF SURE-FIRE MONEY-MAKING IDEAS...

I LIKE THE WAY YOU THINK, TOPH. WHAT'LL IT BE FIRST? THE OL' *"SHELL GAME"*? *"THREE-TILE MONTY"*?

YOU GUYS! WE SAID NO MORE SCAMMING, REMEMBER? I DON'T WANT TO BE CHASED OUT OF ***ANOTHER*** VILLAGE!

HEH, HEH.

THAT'S CERTAINLY NOT HOW I REMEMBER IT!

HELP! HELP! IN THE FOREST!
IT'S A M-M-MONSTER!

WHOOPS, IT'S PROBABLY JUST APPA...I'D BETTER CLEAR THINGS--

UMMF!
QUIET, AANG! DON'T YOU HEAR THAT? IT'S OPPORTUNITY KNOCKING...

THERE WAS THIS LOUD, SCARY ROAR!
THEN SOMETHING HUGE AND FURRY MOVED BEHIND THE BUSHES!
OH, MY STARS! THAT SOUNDS LIKE A FEROCIOUS... SKY BISON!

GOODNESS GRACIOUS! YOU POOR CHILDREN! THAT THING COULD'VE BITTEN OFF YOUR EARS!
SKY BISON? AREN'T THEY EXTINCT?
ARE THEY DANGEROUS? WILL IT ATTACK OUR PEACEFUL VILLAGE?
DIDN'T A SKY BISON ABDUCT YOUR GRANDMOTHER?
DID YOU HEAR? A SKY BISON ABDUCTED MING-MING GRANDMOTHER!
BUT... I'M RIGH HERE.
I'M SORRY TO HEAR ABOUT YOUR GRANDMA, MING-MING...
SOB
I READ SOMEWHERE THAT THEY EAT KITTENS FOR BREAKFAST!
ENOUGH ALREADY, SOKKA! WHAT ARE YOU UP TO?
WATCH AND LEARN, BELOVED SISTER. WATCH AND LEARN.
HOO-BOY! HERE WE GO!
BUT I DON'T THINK I LIKE WHERE THIS IS GOING...

PARDON ME, GOOD CITIZENS. PERHAPS *I* MAY BE OF ASSISTANCE.

I AM SOKKA, **MONSTER SLAYER!**

TAMER OF WILD BEASTS AND ALL FEROCIOUS CREATURES THAT THREATEN PEACEFUL VILLAGES!

OH, MIGHTY WARRIOR-TYPE STRANGER, PLEASE SLAY THE SKY BISON AND BRING MY GRANDMOTHER BACK ALIVE!

HEY! I'M OVER HERE!

FEAR NOT. I WILL PROTECT YOUR PEACEFUL VILLAGE FROM THE RAVENOUS CREATURE LURKING IN THE FOREST...

SHORTLY, IN SAID FOREST...
THERE IS THE MONSTROUS, UM...MONSTER! STAND BACK, VILLAGERS, WHILE I DO MY THIN BUT HAVE THAT MONEY READY. THIS WON'T TAKE LONG...
DON'T FORGET TO RESCUE GRANDMA!
WHAT'S WRONG WITH YOU, GIRL? I'M RIGHT HERE!
KYAI!
AND KYAAAI!
SOME MORE KYAAAAAI!

RRROWRRR

...AN ARMADILLO-BEAR!

THAT THING'S HUGE!
SOKKA IS A GONER! SOB!
WAIT! LOOK! HERE COMES APPA!
GRRRR!
GRRRR!
SCURRY
RRRRROAR!
GO, APPA!
WOOOOSH
KONK

CRRRASHHH
!
ERRRT
WHHHUMP
SNIFF
SNIFF
BE CAREFUL, APPA! IT COULD BE PLAYING *OPOSSUM-BAT!*

HEY...DO YOU GUYS HEAR THAT?

RRRUMBLE

I THINK IT'S SOKKA'S STOMACH!

DO YOU THINK YOU COULD GET APPA TO SHARE SOME OF THAT FOOD?

THE END

DEEP IN THE HEART OF THE FIRE NATION.

UNBELIEVABLE! KATARA AND TOPH DON'T KNOW WHAT THEY'RE MISSING!

I THINK TOPH HAD ENOUGH OF TRAINS IN BA SING SE, AND KATARA SAID SHE WANTED TO RELAX.

BESIDES, APPA'S BEEN LONELY STAYING BEHIND ALL THE TIME.

COMBUSTION MAN ON A TRAIN

Story by Alison Wilgus and Rawles Lumumba, art by Tom McWeeney, colors by Wes Dzioba, and lettering by Comicraft.

OOOOH! I WONDER WHAT THAT'S FOR...AND THAT! AND *THAT!*

WHOOOO WOOOOO!
MY FRIEND GYATSO ONCE TAUGHT ME A TRICK TO HELP ME FEEL BETTER WHEN I WAS SCARED OR NERVOUS. FIRST YOU CLOSE YOUR EYES...

...THEN YOU TAKE DEEP BREATHS AND THINK ABOUT YOUR FAVORITE ANIMAL. KOMODO RHINO, RIGHT?
SEE? THE TRAIN'S NOT SO SCARY NOW.
NO...

BUT SOME OF THE *PEOPLE* STILL ARE. DO YOU KNOW WHY SOMEONE WOULD HAVE A WEIRD SYMBOL ON THEIR HEAD?
OH, I UH... THIS IS JUST...

NOT *YOU,* SILLY. I MEAN *THAT* GUY!

SIR, PLEASE STAY IN YOUR SEAT WHILE I'M COLLECTING TICK--*OOF!*
SHOVE

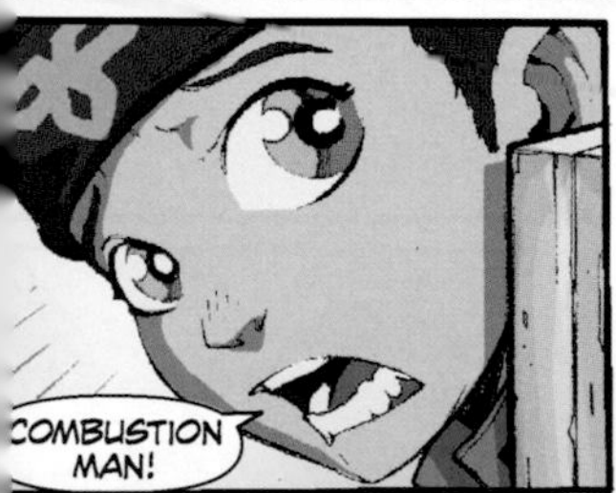
COMBUSTION MAN!

HE MUST HAVE SEEN US AT THE STATION AND FOLLOWED US ONTO THE TRAIN!
WE NEED TO GET OUT OF HERE BEFORE HE SPOTS US! SOMEONE COULD GET HURT.

BOOM

I THINK IT'S A LITTLE LATE FOR THAT!

IT'S *ME* YOU WANT!

YOU DON'T HAVE TO HURT THESE PEOPLE!

KABOOM

FOOOSH

ENGINE ROOM! ENGINE ROOM, WE HAVE AN *EMERGENCY!*

WITH THIS KIND OF DAMAGE, THE TRAIN'S GONNA JUMP THE RAILS! YOU NEED TO STOP IT!
I THINK WE'RE ACTUALLY GOING *FASTER!* AND THE ENGINEER ISN'T RESPONDING!

I'LL TRY TO STOP THE TRAIN WHILE YOU TAKE CARE OF SILENT BUT DEADLY.
GOT IT.

WAIT HERE, SHO, AND STAY OUT OF SIGHT. I HAVE TO TAKE CARE OF THIS.
BUT REMEMBER THE BREATHING EXERCISES, OKAY?

O-OKAY...

HRRRR!
AANG!
TAP

WHOOSH
SMASH

GASP!

SWOOOSH

DEEP BREATHS! DON'T FORGET THE TECHNIQUE!
WHOOSH

WOW!
WHOOSH

LOOKING FOR SOMEONE?

FWISH
YOU'RE GONNA HAVE TO COME UP HERE TO GET A BETTER SHOT!

GRUNT

KRAKOOM

WHISH

CLANG

EEP!
THUMP

STOP THE TRAIN! EMERGENCY! CAN'T YOU HEAR THE EXPLOSIONS?!
BANG
BANG
KABOOOOOM

MAN, I REALLY WISH TOPH WAS HERE...

CLANG
I MAY NOT BE ABLE TO *METALBEND...*

...BUT I CAN *BEND METAL!*
CREEEEEEEEK

HE MUST'VE HIT HIS HEAD DURING ONE OF THE EXPLOSIONS.

IT CAN'T BE *THAT* HARD TO DRIVE THIS THING, RIGHT?

WHOOSH
SCREEEEEEEEE
BOOM
FOOSH

RUMBLE RUMBLE
≶GASP!≷
WAAAAH!!
YOU JUST HAVE TO RELAX!
TAKE DEEP BREATHS, AND IMAGINE THERE'S A *GIANT* KOMODO RHINO THAT WON'T LET *ANYTHING* HURT YOU.
JUST *RELAX.*
CAN IT BE A GIANT MEER-PENGUIN *INSTEAD?!* THEY'RE REALLY CUTE!

BOOM
A GUY CAN'T EVEN GET A MINUTE TO CONCENTRATE.
YOU'D THINK THEY'D MAKE THE EMERGENCY BRAKE EASIER TO FIND.
CLANG
"FINE FIRE NATION CRAFTSMANSHIP" MY WOLFTAIL!
UGH! HERE WE GO!
CLANK
SCREEEEEEEE
WHOOOOA!
WHISH
WHEW!

FOOOSH
!
SPLISH
UGH. W-WHAT HAPPENED? I WAS TRYING TO STOP THE TRAIN, AND THEN THERE WAS THIS BIG EXPLOSION.
NO WORRIES! I TOOK CARE OF IT!
IN THAT CASE...KEEP THE HAT.
IS EVERYONE OKAY?
YOU WERE RIGHT...

...THOSE BREATHING EXERCISES REALLY *DO* WORK.

YOU DID GREAT, SHO!
THANKS, BUT...THE TRAIN LOOKS PRETTY BROKEN AND I'M SUPPOSED TO BE AT MY GRANDMA'S HOUSE FOR DINNER!

SHO, I'D LIKE YOU TO MEET *MY* FAVORITE ANIMAL. HE CAN TAKE YOU TO YOUR GRAN'S HOUSE!

DEEP BREATHS...DEEP BREATHS...

THE END

Story by Alison Wilgus, art by Justin Ridge, colors by Wes Dzioba, and lettering by Comicraft.

YOU KNOW, LIKE AN AGNI KAI, ONLY WITH SWORDS INSTEAD OF FIRE--
YEAH, I GET IT!

BUT THERE'S NO SUCH THING AS A "SWORDBENDING KAI."

SIGH
BUT HONOR DEMANDS THAT I ACCEPT YOUR CHALLENGE.
WOO!

MOMENTS LATER...
FINALLY! SOME ACTION AROUND HERE!
DON'T GET YOUR HOPES UP, SOKKA. I STARTED TRAINING WITH MASTER PIANDAO WHEN I WAS JUST A KID...
...SO I THINK I CAN TAKE A BEGINNER LIKE YOU.

ALL RIGHT, YOU GUYS. I WANT A GOOD, CLEAN SWORDBENDING MATCH!
THERE'S NO SUCH THING!
FWEEEEEEEET
SO YOU THINK YOU'RE *HOT STUFF*, HUH?

LIKE I SAID...
SWISH

WHOA!
WOOSH

OOF!
BAM

...DON'T GET YOUR HOPES UP.
REMATCH. NOW.

ANOTHER LOSS FOR SOKKA!
THUMP
AND SO ON...
OUCH.
BAM

THIS IS RIDICULOUS. I'M OBVIOUSLY BETTER THAN YOU. WHY DON'T YOU JUST GIVE UP?

THIS FROM THE GUY WHO UNSUCCESSFULLY HUNTED AANG FOR THREE YEARS?
THAT WAS TOTALLY DIFFERENT!
SURE...

...'CAUSE IT'LL ONLY TAKE THREE MINUTES TO BEAT YOU!

TING
YOU WERE SAYING?

HYAH!

WHOOSH
HEY! NO BOOMERANGS I[N] SWORDBENDING!

WHISH WHISH WHISH WHISH WHISH
WAIT...
...I MEAN--

KLONK

ZUKO'S RIGHT, YOU KNOW. YOU DID CHEAT, SO HE STILL WINS THE MATCH.
I MAY HAVE LOST THE BATTLE OF SWORDS, YOUNG AVATAR...

...BUT I WON THE BATTLE OF WORDS.
HMPH.
THE END

Story by Alison Wilgus, art by Elsa Garagarza, colors by Wes Dzioba, and lettering by Comicraft.

THAT NIGHT...
WHOA!
WAS THAT THERE WHEN WE LEFT?
PLEASE DO COME IN, LORD MOMO.
WE'VE BEEN KEEPING YOUR HAT WARM FOR YOU.

OH, SO SORRY! BUT I'M AFRAID YOU CAN'T COME IN.
BUT YOU LET MOMO IN!
OF COURSE! HE ISN'T A BENDER. AND THIS IS A STRICTLY BEND-FREE ESTABLISHMENT.

HEY! LEAVE SOME LYCHEE NUTS FOR ME!
DON'T LET HIM GET TO YOU, AANG! WE'RE AT WAR. WE HAVE TO TRAIN.
IT'S NOT YOUR FAULT HE'S BEING SUCH A BABY ABOUT IT.

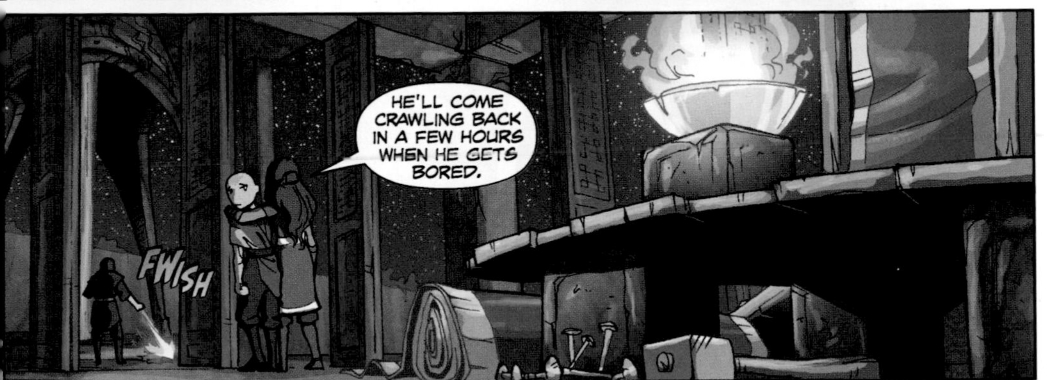
HE'LL COME CRAWLING BACK IN A FEW HOURS WHEN HE GETS BORED.
FWISH

LET THE FIRST MEETING OF THE BENDLESS BOOMERANGERS CLUB COMMENCE!

BEVERAGES AND SNACKS WILL BE SERVED IN THE MAIN HALL, FOLLOWED BY ADVANCED BOOMERANG LESSONS IN THE FOYER!
HE NEVER SHOWED **ME** HOW TO USE A BOOMERANG...
AANG, YOU CAN THROW ROCKS ***WITH YOUR MIND!***
STILL...
WHUP WHUP

WHUP WHUP
HEY! WHAT'S THAT!?
SNATCH

WOW, THIS WENT A LONG WAY!
COME ON, LET'S GO BACK AND TEST OUT THE OTHER ONES I MADE!
SO CLOSE...

DID YOU SEE THAT AWESOME TOY?
NOPE.

WE HAVE TO GET INTO THAT CLUBHOUSE!
WHY? IT'S JUST A BUNCH OF STUPID KIDDIE STUFF.

BUT THEY HAVE FLYING TOYS!
YOU'RE AN AIRBENDER.
AND HATS!
AANG, YOU'RE THE AVATAR. I THINK YOU'VE GOT MORE IMPORTANT THINGS TO WORRY ABOUT.

YOU'RE RIGHT. IT'S STUPID. I DON'T NEED TO BE IN SOME SILLY CLUB.
GET SOME SLEEP, OKAY? I BET YOU'LL FEEL BETTER ABOUT IT IN THE MORNING.
SIGH

BUT THE NEXT MORNING...
PLEASE, PLEASE, PLEASE LET ME INTO YOUR CLUB!
WELL... I SUPPOSE I CAN MAKE ANOTHER EXCEPTION...

ANOTHER?!
I THOUGHT YOU GUYS SAID THIS WAS DUMB KIDS' STUFF?
UH... WELL, THEY'RE HAVING A PAI SHO TOURNAMENT, AND IT'S UM... WHAT UNCLE WOULD WANT?
FREE FOOT MASSAGES TWICE A WEEK. ENOUGH SAID.
AND YOU KNOW... THE HATS.

WELL, I'M GLAD YOU LET US BENDERS JOIN YOUR CLUB, SOKKA. IT'S PRETTY GREAT!
OF COURSE, OF COURSE. ALTHOUGH... YOU DO STILL HAVE TO RECITE THE BOOMERANGER OATH.

I PLEDGE ALLEGIANCE TO MY BENDLESS BRETHREN, AND ADMIT THAT NO BENDING CAN EQUAL THE MIGHT OF THE NOBLE BOOMERANG. ONE TEAM, UNDER HATS, INDIVISIBLE, WITH SNACKS AND FIELD TRIPS FOR ALL.
THE END

Story by J. Torres, art and colors by Gurihiru, and lettering by Comicraft.

THINK FAST!
WHAT THE--?!
SPLOOOSHH
HA HA HA! ⇉SNORT!⇇ HEE HEE!
THAT'S IT? THAT'S WHAT YOU HAD TO SAY TO ME? I THOUGHT MAYBE YOU *FINALLY* WANTED TO TALK ABOUT--
ENOUGH MOPING AROUND. TIME TO PRACTICE YOUR FIREBENDING.
WATCH OUT OR YOU MIGHT GET ANOTHER ONE IN THE *KISSER*...
KISS...

...ERR...
EVERYTHING'S GOING TO BE DIFFERENT AFTER TODAY, ISN'T IT?
YES, IT IS.
WHAT IF... WHAT IF I DON'T COME BACK?
KISS...
...HER...
AANG, DON'T SAY THAT. OF COURSE YOU'LL--
COME ON, AANG! ZUKO SAID TO PRACTICE YOUR FIREBENDING WHILE HE'S AWAY WITH SOKKA!
HUH? WHAT?

AANG, YOU HAVE TO BE READY TO BATTLE THE *FIRE LORD.* THIS IS NO TIME FOR GAMES OR PLAYING "HIDE-*AANG*-SEEK."

WHO'S *REALLY* PLAYING GAMES HERE, KATARA? ARE YOU SURE YOU'RE NOT THE ONE HIDING... *SOMETHING?* I THOUGHT YOU WANTED TO TALK ABOUT WHAT HAPPENED BEFORE THE INVASION!

UH... I DON'T KNOW WHAT YOU'RE TALKING ABOUT...

I MEAN... I CAN'T HEAR YOU PROPERLY FROM IN THERE SO, *UM...*

...JUST COME OUT AND BRING THE *HEAT!*

HA! OBVIOUSLY, *YOU* CAN'T HANDLE IT WHEN THINGS GET A LITTLE TOO *HOT!*

THIS ISN'T ABOUT US...I MEAN, ME...I MEAN, YOU...I MEAN, YOU'RE SUPPOSED TO BE PREPARING FOR THE FIRE LORD!
SHUNK
SHUNK
CUT IT OUT, KATARA! I SAID I DON'T FEEL LIKE DOING THIS RIGHT NOW!
COME ON ALREADY, AANG! SHOW ME SOME FIRE!
FINE! YOU WANT FIRE? I'LL SHOW YOU FIRE!!!
FWWOOOSSSH
WHOA!

KRRRAAAK
OH, NO!
KATARA!
I'M SO SORRY! I DIDN'T MEAN TO HURT YOU... ARE YOU OKAY?
I'M FINE, AANG--AND THAT "VOLCANO" MOVE WAS IMPRESSIVE!
COME ON, LET'S PRACTICE IT AGAIN SO YOU CAN SHOW ZUKO LATER...
WHERE ARE YOU GOING? ARE YOU...SCARED OF BURNING ME AGAIN?
ACTUALLY...
...I'M MORE WORRIED ABOUT BEING THE ONE WHO GETS BURNED.
NOT THE EN

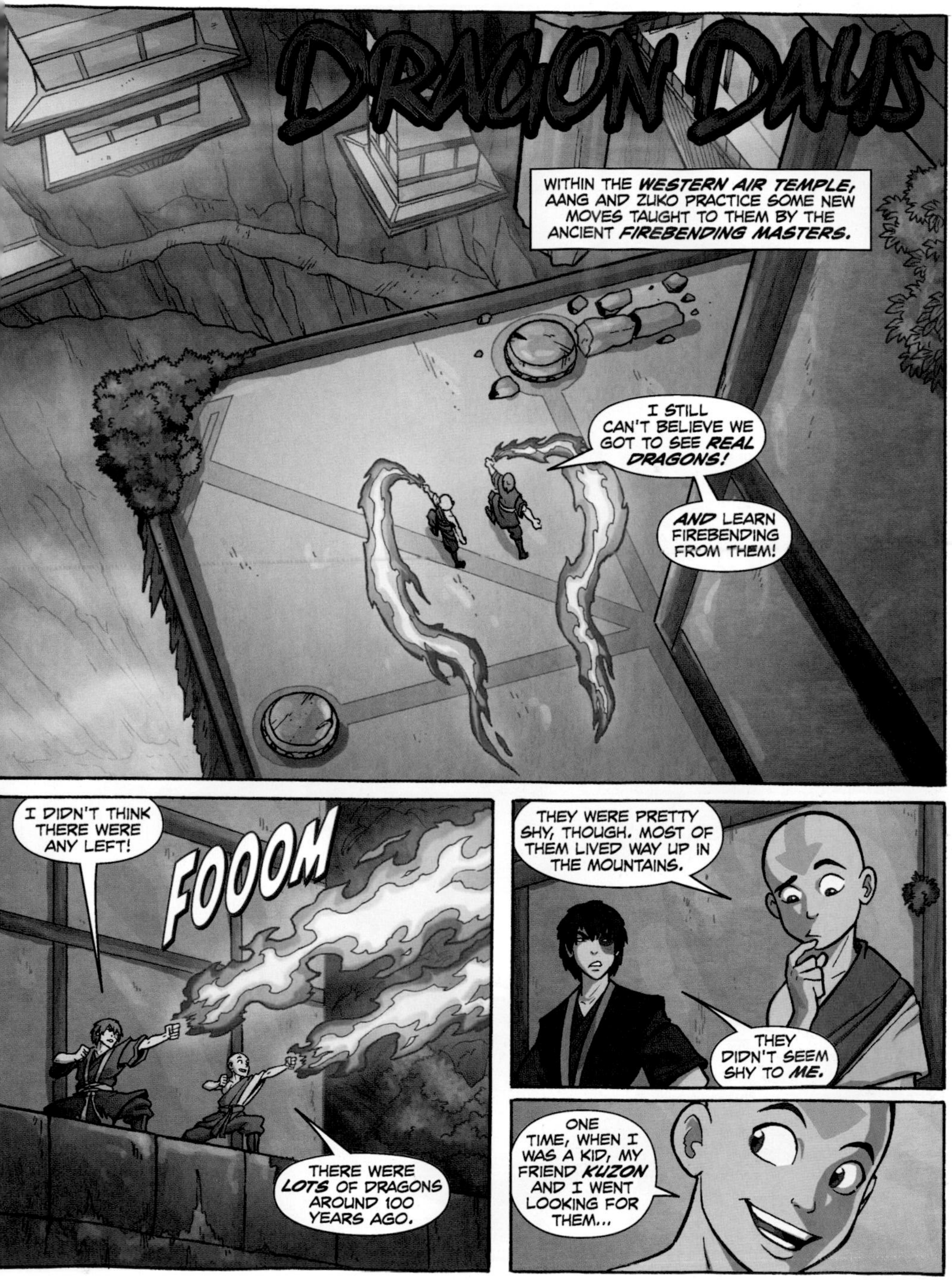

DRAGON DAYS

WITHIN THE ***WESTERN AIR TEMPLE,*** AANG AND ZUKO PRACTICE SOME NEW MOVES TAUGHT TO THEM BY THE ANCIENT ***FIREBENDING MASTERS.***

I STILL CAN'T BELIEVE WE GOT TO SEE ***REAL DRAGONS!***

AND LEARN FIREBENDING FROM THEM!

I DIDN'T THINK THERE WERE ANY LEFT!
FOOOM
THERE WERE ***LOTS*** OF DRAGONS AROUND 100 YEARS AGO.

THEY WERE PRETTY SHY, THOUGH. MOST OF THEM LIVED WAY UP IN THE MOUNTAINS.
THEY DIDN'T SEEM SHY TO ***ME.***
ONE TIME, WHEN I WAS A KID, MY FRIEND ***KUZON*** AND I WENT LOOKING FOR THEM...

Story by Alison Wilgus, art by Johane Matte (frame) and Tom McWeeney (flashback), colors by Wes Dzioba, and lettering by Comicraft.

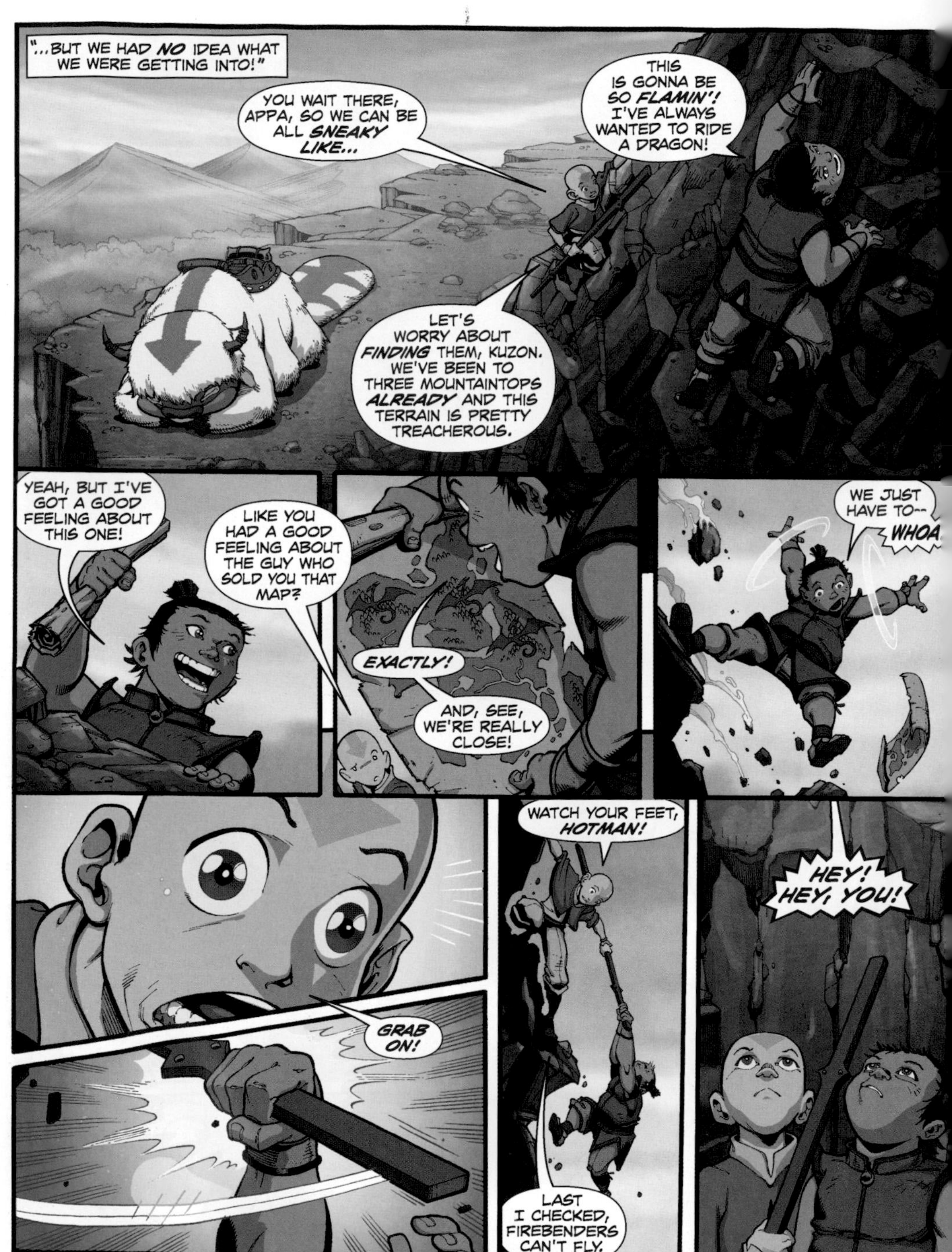
"...BUT WE HAD NO IDEA WHAT WE WERE GETTING INTO!"
YOU WAIT THERE, APPA, SO WE CAN BE ALL SNEAKY LIKE...
THIS IS GONNA BE SO FLAMIN'! I'VE ALWAYS WANTED TO RIDE A DRAGON!
LET'S WORRY ABOUT FINDING THEM, KUZON. WE'VE BEEN TO THREE MOUNTAINTOPS ALREADY AND THIS TERRAIN IS PRETTY TREACHEROUS.
YEAH, BUT I'VE GOT A GOOD FEELING ABOUT THIS ONE!
LIKE YOU HAD A GOOD FEELING ABOUT THE GUY WHO SOLD YOU THAT MAP?
EXACTLY!
AND, SEE, WE'RE REALLY CLOSE!
WE JUST HAVE TO--
GRAB ON!
WATCH YOUR FEET, HOTMAN!
LAST I CHECKED, FIREBENDERS CAN'T FLY.
HEY! HEY, YOU!

COME ON...
...DON'T BE SHY!

I KNOW YOU CAN SEE ME...

...HEH, HEH. OR SMELL ME!
HA! I KNOW YOU'RE TRYING TO SNEAK UP ON ME...
...GOOD LUCK WITH THAT!

RRRRRRRRR

GIDDYUP!

WHOA! LOOK AT HIM GO! I WONDER WHAT HE'S RUNNING--

WHOOOOOOSH
--FROM?!?
RRRRRRG!
OH, MAN, OH, MAN, OH, MAN, OH, MAN!
SNAP
I'M GOING AFTER HIM. HE COULD BE IN TROUBLE!
WAIT...
...DO YOU HEAR THAT?
!
I CAN'T BELIEVE THIS TWO-BIT MAP WAS ACTUALLY ***LEGIT.***
TOLD YA. YOU GOTTA TRUST PEOPLE MORE.
VERY NICE. THIS ONE WILL FETCH QUITE A PRICE ON THE BLACK MARKET...

THAT GUY WASN'T IN TROUBLE! HE JUST WANTED TO LURE THE MOM AWAY FROM HER EGG!

WHAT'RE WE GONNA DO? WE CAN'T LET THEM GET AWAY WITH IT!
WE *WON'T.*

IF WE JUST RUSH UP THERE AND FIGHT THEM, WE MIGHT HURT THE EGG.

BUT MAYBE...

UP FOR SOME BENDING, *MY GOOD HOTMAN?*
YOU KNOW IT!

ROOOOARR

ROOOOAR!
WHOOSH
WHOOSH

COULD SHE BE BACK ALREADY?

FSSSST
THESE FIREBALLS ARE WAY TOO WIMPY LOOKING...

NEED A HAND, HOTMAN?

FOOOOM
FLAME-E-O!

FOOOM
AHHH!
MAAAH! MAAAH!

RUN!

DON'T WORRY, LITTLE GUY!

I'VE GOT--

WHOA!
MAAAH!

WHEW!

GROAN...
UH-OH.

UMM... I KNOW THIS LOOKS BAD, MRS. DRAGON, BUT I WAS ACTUALLY TRYING TO...

GRRRRRRRRR
HEY!

FWOOSH
OVER HERE, YOU BIG CHICKEN-LIZARD!

SWOOSH
RRR?
EEP! OH, DEAR...

OOF!
FWIP
BAM
WHOOSH
WHEW! THANK GOODNESS FOR EXTRA-PADDED ARMOR!
GULP

SLUUURRP
HEY, IT'S NO PROBLEM!

WE COULDN'T LET ANYTHING HAPPEN TO YOUR BABY.
SO, UHH... MAYBE YOU COULD GIVE US A RIDE AS A REWARD?

YOU KNOW... JUST A COUPLE OF LAPS AROUND THE MOUNTAIN?
THAT WOULD BE HOT! FLAMIN' HOT!

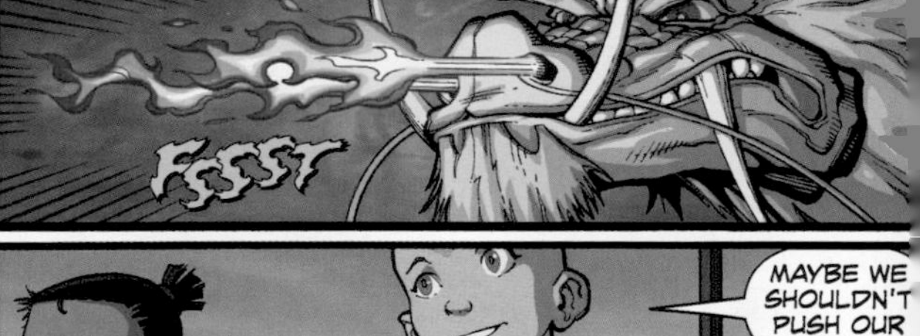
FSSST

MAYBE WE SHOULDN'T PUSH OUR LUCK.

=SIGH= A LOT SURE HAS CHANGED SINCE THOSE DAYS...
YEAH. LIKE THE SLANG.
WHATEVER, SIFU HOTMAN.
STOP CALLING ME THAT!
THE END

Story by Katie Mattila, art by Justin Ridge, colors by Hye Jung Kim, and lettering by Comicraft.

I THINK WE'RE GOING TO MAKE A GREAT TEAM, MOMO. NOW, WHERE DO YOU SUSPECT AANG IS HIDING?
CHITTER CHITTER
YOU'D BETTER BE LEADING ME IN THE RIGHT DIRECTION, MOMO!

HEY! MOMO HELPED YOU. THAT'S NOT FAIR!
THAT'S DETECTIVE MOMO TO YOU!
NICE WORK, BUDDY.

HMMM.
THESE FOOTPRINTS SEEM TO BE THE EXACT SIZE OF KATARA'S FEET.
AND THEY SEEM TO END RIGHT NEAR THAT WATERFALL.

=SIGH= THAT WAS WAY TOO EASY.

YAHHHHH!

WHAT WAS THAT?
HA! GOT YOU! I WIN HIDE-AND-SHRIEK!

IT'S HIDE-AND-SEEK, ZUKO.
I GOT YOU.

I REALLY HATE GAMES.

UH, NICE TRY, APPA.
ALMOST DIDN'T SEE YOU THERE.

SLUUURP

I GUESS WE MIGHT AS WELL GO FIND TOPH AND FINISH THE GAME...
SQUEAKASQUEAK!

BUT TIME PASSES...
WELL, WE'VE NARROWED IT DOWN TO THIS AREA... BUT WHY HAVEN'T WE FOUND HER YET?
SKREE?

OUR DETECTIVE SKILLS ARE SUPERB...

...THIS DOESN'T MAK SENSE.

SMASH
CRUMBLE
I CAN'T STAND IT ANY LONGER!!!

SORRY...BUT YOU REALLY NEED TO CLEAN THOSE FEET OF YOURS--THEY STINK!
GOT YOU...
PLOP
GAME OVER!

Bumi vs. Toph Round 1

THE AVATAR'S FRIENDS HIDE OUT AMONG THE ORDER OF THE WHITE LOTUS IN "OLD PEOPLE CAMP," AWAITING BATTLE WITH THE DREADED FIRE LORD.

⇉YAWN!⇇

I STILL CAN'T BELIEVE YOU RETOOK OMASHU FROM THE FIRE NATION ALL BY YOURSELF. YOU REALLY MUST BE THE GREATEST EARTHBENDER OF ALL TIME!

THAT'S RIGHT.

Story by Johane Matte and Joshua Hamilton, art by Johane Matte, colors by Hye Jung Kim, and lettering by Comicraft.

HMMPH.
NO OFFENSE, POPS, BUT JUST BECAUSE YOU'RE AS OLD AS DIRT DOESN'T MEAN YOU KNOW HOW TO BEND IT!
LITTLE GIRL, I HAVE TOENAILS THAT CAN EARTHBEND BETTER THAN YOU.
OH, REALLY?!
THAT'S RIGHT!
THERE'S ONLY ONE SURE WAY TO FIND OUT WHO'S THE BETTER EARTHBENDER...
...AN EARTHBENDING RUMBLE!!!

I WANT A NICE, MESSY, ROCK-FILLED FIGHT!
AND, IN THE WEST CORNER OF THE CANYON, WE HAVE KING BUMI, A.K.A. THE *MAD EARTHBENDING GENIUS,* A.K.A. THE *OVER-THE-HILL HITTER.*
IN THE EAST CORNER, WE HAVE TOPH, A.K.A. *THE BLIND BANDIT,* A.K.A. *THE RUNAWAY,* SELF-PROCLAIMED GREATEST EARTHBENDER OF ALL TIME!
OKAY, BENDERS, WE'LL START AT THE GONG.
BONG!

?!?
YOUNG PEOPLE GO FIRST...
I WOULDN'T DREAM OF BEING DISRESPECTFUL TO MY ELDER...
COME ON, ALREADY! FIGHT!!!

GO, BLIND BANDIT! SHOW THAT OLD-TIMER WHO'S BOSS!

GO, MAD GENIUS! TEACH THAT YOUNGSTER A THING OR TWO!

RUMBLE
BOOM
WHAT'S GOING ON?
JUST THE MATCH DECIDING WHO IS THE ULTIMATE EARTHBENDER OF ALL TIME!
YOU'RE LETTING THEM BATTLE EACH OTHER?! WHAT IF THEY GET HURT? YOU REALIZE WE'RE ABOUT TO FACE THE FIRE NATION, AND THE FATE OF THE WORLD RESTS IN OUR HANDS?!
DON'T WORRY, KATARA, I WON'T HURT HIM! JUST GOTTA TEST TO MAKE SURE THE OLD GUY CAN ACTUALLY SURVIVE ANOTHER FIGHT WITH THOSE FIREBENDERS.
AND I'M MAKING SURE THE LITTLE GIRL WON'T GET BURNED TOO MUCH.

ROCKALANCHE! NICE!
RUMBLE!

CRRACK!!

!?
TREMBLE

TREMBLE
SPLAT

TREMBLE
WHAT'S HAPPENING?!

LOOKS LIKE I WON!

ARE WE UNDER ATTACK?!
WHERE ARE THE KIDS?!

I'LL FIND THEM!
I JUST HOPE I'M NOT *TOO LATE!*

WHAT THE--?
EXPLAIN YOURSELVES!
BRAKABOOM
IT'S THE ULTIMATE EARTHBENDING SHOWDOWN! TWO OPPOSING STYLES! TWO OPPOSING AGE GROUPS! ONE WINNER!

YOU'VE *GOT* TO BE KIDDING ME.
GO, BUMI! OLD PEOPLE, *REPRESENT!*

I DON'T THINK THIS BENDING BATTLE IS SUCH A GOOD IDEA. IT COULD GIVE AWAY OUR LOCATION.
YEAH, AREN'T WE SUPPOSED TO BE HIDING?
CRASH!
*HMM...*YOU HAVE A POINT.

THE ULTIMATE BENDING BATTLE IS OFFICIALLY OVER!
BONG! BONG! BONG!
FWAP

I DON'T THINK THEY CAN HEAR THE BELL.
OH, REALLY?

I GUESS WE'LL HAVE TO STOP IT, BENDER STYLE!

THIS IS GETTING REALLY GOOD!

ALL RIGHT! BREAK IT UP!
FWOOOSH
SHOW'S OVER!
≠COUGH≠

SO WHO WON, ANYWAY?
AS REFEREE, I HAVE TO SAY IT WAS A DRAW.
BOTH OF YOU NEED TO START ACTING YOUR AGE.
PHPTHH.

WE'LL JUST HAVE TO HAVE A REMATCH LATER.
SWEET!
HEH HEH! ≠SNORT!≠
THE END

BONUS STORIES

Story by Dave Roman, art by Justin Ridge, colors by Sno Cone Studios and Hye Jung Kim, and lettering by Comicraft.

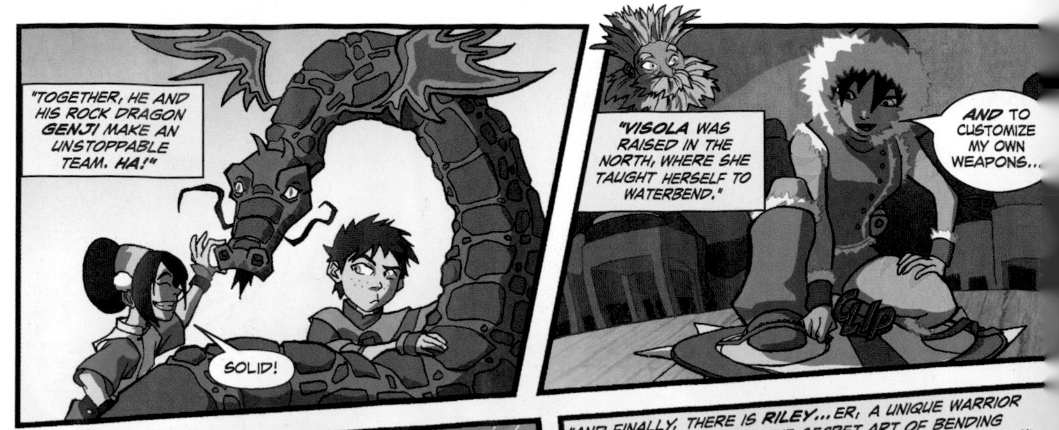
"TOGETHER, HE AND HIS ROCK DRAGON GENJI MAKE AN UNSTOPPABLE TEAM. HA!"
SOLID!
"VISOLA WAS RAISED IN THE NORTH, WHERE SHE TAUGHT HERSELF TO WATERBEND."
AND TO CUSTOMIZE MY OWN WEAPONS...
CHIP

...LIKE MY WAVE RING!
YOU GOTTA LET ME RIDE THAT!
SPLASH

"AND FINALLY, THERE IS RILEY... ER, A UNIQUE WARRIOR WHO HAS MASTERED THE SECRET ART OF BENDING ...COOKIE DOUGH!"

MMM... TALK ABOUT SKILLS TO PAY THE BILLS!
SIGH

THE GANG DEBATES IN PRIVATE.
SHOULD WE TAKE A VOTE?
WE SHOULD ONLY CHOOSE THE BEST OF THE BEST...
MY STOMACH ALREADY VOTED.

AFTER THE VOTE...
WAIT! WHERE ARE THEY GOING?
I GUESS THEY DIDN'T LIKE BEING JUDGED.
EXIT
THEY WENT OFF TO FORM THEIR OWN GANG. HA!
THE END

Story by Alison Wilgus, art by Ethan Spaulding, colors by Wes Dzioba, and lettering by Comicraft.

選擇我
Pick Me!
MAI.
WHATEVER.
WHAT AM I SUPPOSED TO DO, THEN?!
YOU'RE THE BALL.
BAM
WHOOSH
THE END!

ABOUT THE CREATORS

BRYAN KONIETZKO & MICHAEL DANTE DIMARTINO, the cocreators of *Avatar: The Last Airbender*, met at a Halloween party in 1995, and have been friends and creative partners ever since. They've worn many hats over the course of *Avatar*'s production, working not only as the show's executive producers but also as its writers, directors, story editors, and artists. And their hands-on approach to creating the series doesn't stop there—they've traveled the world taking reference photos for their artists, and have spent months in South Korea making sure their overseas animators are as involved in the creative process as the folks working out of their Los Angeles studio. Bryan and Mike are currently hard at work creating *Airbender*'s sequel series, *Legend of Korra.*

AARON EHASZ served as head writer and coproducer of many of *Avatar: The Last Airbender*'s most memorable episodes, including "Jet," "The Blind Bandit," "The Tales of Ba Sing Se," and the four-part series finale, "Sozin's Comet." He's also written episodes of *Mission Hill, Ed,* and *Futurama.*

ALISON WILGUS most recently wrote *Zuko's Story*, a graphic-novel prequel about the prince of the Fire Nation, with coconspirator Dave Roman. In addition to writing comics for *Nickelodeon Magazine* based on *Avatar: The Last Airbender*, she's to blame for several episodes of *Codename: Kids Next Door*, and is currently wrapping up volume 1 of her original comic, *Chronin.*

One of the winners of Tokyopop's fourth Rising Stars of Manga competition, **AMY KIM GANTER**'s comics work includes an adaptation of the *Goosebumps* story "Deep Trouble," two stories for the acclaimed comics anthology *Flight*, and the graphic-novel series *Sorcerers & Secretaries.*

BRIAN RALPH, the award-winning creator of the graphic novels *Cave-In* and *Climbing Out*, teaches at the Savannah College of Art and Design, which has one of the largest and best-known sequential-art departments in the United States.

CLEM ROBINS started lettering comics in 1977, back when it was all done by hand. On top of being a very talented letterer, he's also an artist. He's taught at the Art Academy of Cincinnati and wrote *The Art of Figure Drawing* (2002).

Richard Starkings's award-winning studio **COMICRAFT** has been providing the comics community with fine lettering since 1992. Best known for pioneering the use of computers in comic-book lettering, Comicraft has not only lettered hundreds of comics, but has also designed some of the industry's most popular fonts.

COREY LEWIS has created lots of great comics, but he's probably best known for *Sharknife*, the story of a busboy at a Chinese restaurant who transforms into a mighty warrior to battle the monsters that live in the restaurant's walls (providing no end of entertainment for their customers!).

DAVE ROMAN, the award-winning author of *Astronaut Academy: Zero Gravity*, has had a long relationship with *Airbender*—as the comics editor of *Nickelodeon Magazine* for over ten years, he looked after the very first *Airbender* comics. More recently, he's been involved with *Airbender* as cowriter of the movie tie-in graphic novels *Zuko's Story* and *The Last Airbender.*

ELSA GARAGARZA is the concept artist and designer behind many of *Avatar: The Last Airbender*'s most exciting locations. She's also a storyboard artist, and has worked on projects like the *Penguins of Madagascar* TV series, *Green Lantern: First Flight*, and *Generator Rex*.

ETHAN SPAULDING directed twelve episodes of *Avatar: The Last Airbender*, and worked on many more as a storyboard artist, character designer, and background artist. He's also worked on *The Simpsons* and *Green Lantern: First Flight*, and is currently working as a producer on *ThunderCats*.

FRANK PITTARESE has been writing and editing comics since the 1980s, working on titles like *The Flash*, *Superman*, and *X-Men*, and worked as a freelancer for *Nickelodeon Magazine*, where he edited and wrote articles, activities, and comics featuring almost all of their characters, from Rugrats to SpongeBob SquarePants.

Teaming up under the name **GURIHIRU**, Japanese artists Sasaki and Kawano create artwork for comics, games, and animation studios. They've recently been doing a lot of work for Marvel, drawing and coloring *Thor and the Warriors Four*, *Power Pack*, *Tails of the Pet Avengers*, and *World War Hulks: Wolverine vs. Captain America*.

HYE JUNG KIM worked on *Avatar: The Last Airbender* as a painter, artist, and color supervisor, using her talents to help create the show's rich settings and exotic environments. She's also worked her artistic magic on *Dora the Explorer*, *The Fairly OddParents*, *Young Justice*, *G.I. Joe: Resolute*, and *Green Lantern: First Flight*.

Creator of the award-winning series *Alison Dare*, **J. TORRES** has also written *Batman: Legends of the Dark Knight*, *WALL-E*, *Teen Titans Go!*, and *Wonder Girl* comics. He's written for animation too, on series like *Hi Hi Puffy AmiYumi*, *Edgar & Ellen*, and *League of Super Evil*, and is currently writing *Jinx* for Archie Comics.

JOAQUIM DOS SANTOS came to *Airbender* as a storyboard artist, but became a director on season three episodes like "The Day of Black Sun Part 2: The Eclipse" and "Sozin's Comet Part 3: Into the Inferno." He's since directed many other projects, including *G.I. Joe: Resolute*, but has returned to *Airbender* as co-executive producer of the sequel series, *Legend of Korra*. Joaquim has been nicknamed "Dr. Fight" because of his talent for choreographing dynamic action scenes.

Another veteran of the *Flight* comics anthology, **JOHANE MATTE** worked on *Avatar: The Last Airbender* as a storyboard artist. She's currently a storyboard artist at DreamWorks Animation, where she's worked on *How to Train Your Dragon*, and the upcoming *Rise of the Guardians* (2012).

JOHN O'BRYAN was a staff writer for *Avatar: The Last Airbender*, and wrote many episodes, including "The King of Omashu," "Avatar Day," and "Nightmares and Daydreams."

JOSHUA HAMILTON started on *Airbender* as a writer's assistant, but rose to become a full writer during the show's production, writing episodes like "The Painted Lady" and "The Runaway."

JUSTIN RIDGE worked as a storyboard artist on *Avatar: The Last Airbender*, and later worked as a storyboard artist for *G.I. Joe: Resolute* and as a director and storyboard artist on *Star Wars: The Clone Wars*. He currently works as a guest director on *The Cleveland Show*. His comics work has appeared in *Zombies vs. Cheerleaders*, *Flight*, and *Shojo Beat*.

KATIE MATTILA started out as a production assistant on *Airbender*, but grew to become a production coordinator and ultimately a writer's assistant for the show, and wrote the episode "The Beach." She's currently working on the series *Kung Fu Panda: Legends of Awesomeness.*

As part of the Nickelodeon Writing Fellowship, **MAY CHAN** spent a lot of time in the writing room of the *Avatar: The Last Airbender* animated series, eventually writing part one of "The Boiling Rock." She also wrote for the Disney series *Phineas and Ferb.*

RAWLES LUMUMBA is a freelance writer and native of Baltimore, Maryland. In addition to comics, she is an author of fantasy and sci-fi young-adult fiction. She also blogs about diversity in television, video games, and pop culture.

REAGAN LODGE got his start as a contributing artist on the acclaimed *Flight* anthology series, for which he created "Tea" and "The Dragon." He currently serves in the US Marine Corps as a combat photographer, but don't worry: he still draws too.

SNO CONE STUDIOS colored and lettered a wide variety of comic series, including *Star Wars*, *Teen Titans*, *Hawkman*, *Legion of Super-Heroes*, *Shrek*, and *Scooby-Doo.* Though they've now closed up shop, their work is still enjoyed by comics fans to this day.

A writer for the *Avatar: The Last Airbender* animated series, **TIM HEDRICK** authored such episodes as "The Deserter," "Sokka's Master," and "The Puppetmaster."

TOM McWEENEY has written, drawn, and lettered comics since the 1980s. He cocreated *Roachmill* and has contributed to a number of other titles, including *Teenage Mutant Ninja Turtles*, *Fantastic Four*, and *Gen13.*

WES DZIOBA has been coloring comics for over a decade, getting his start at comics-coloring studios but then moving on as an independent colorist on books like *Star Wars*; *Magnus, Robot Fighter*; and *Aliens vs. Predator: Three World War.*

THE ART OF THE ANIMATED SERIES

When we created *Avatar: The Last Airbender* in 2002, we set out to tell a story with integrity and heart. We wanted *Avatar* to connect with people of all ages, all around the world, but it is still humbling and amazing to us that the show did just that!

A big part of the reason is the beautiful artwork. The following pages hold just a small example of the tens of thousands of storyboards, designs, paintings, and animation drawings that were created for *Avatar*. Much more can be found in *Avatar: The Last Airbender—The Art of the Animated Series*. This is a very personal book written by us for the fans of the show. In it, we take you from the first sketch of Aang, through the entire production, explaining firsthand how the concept and characters were created. It is a unique look into the development and production process of the series, and we are proud to showcase so much of the amazing work that was produced by our artists in Los Angeles and South Korea.

We hope you enjoy this preview of *Avatar: The Last Airbender—The Art of the Animated Series*.

—Bryan Konietzko & Michael Dante DiMartino

After JM Animation showed us some early season-one pencil tests, we were impressed by how much life the animators breathed into the characters. Here are Bryan's studies of their work, along with some of his own Sokka expressions.

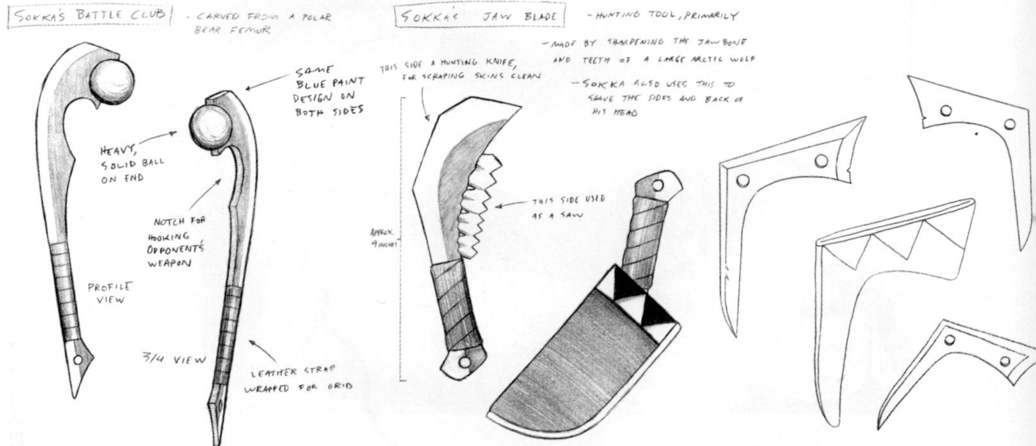

Sokka's club, knife, and signature boomerang. These Water Tribe props, crafted from bone and leather, were inspired by traditional Native American weapons. Designs by Bryan Konietzko.

Aang key animation by Ryu Ki Hyun.

Exploring the many moods of Katara, from vulnerable young girl to commanding parental presence. Series bible sketches by Bryan Konietzko.

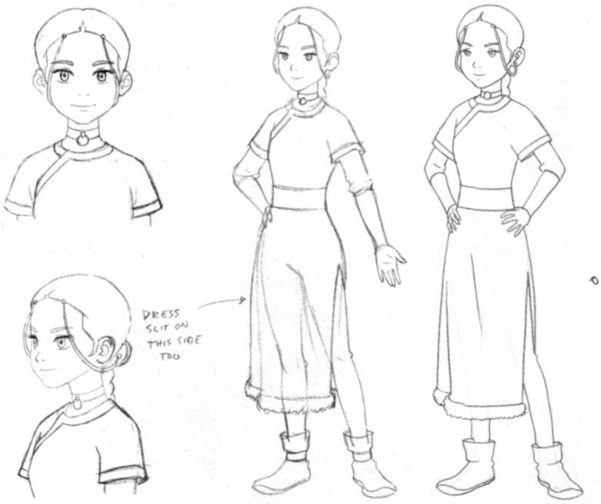

Bryan and Yoon Young Ki worked together on Katara's design for the pilot.

Katara expressions by Bryan from early in season one. Many of these poses are studies of the great work we saw coming back from JM Animation.

This design depicts the trench that the townsfolk created to protect the village from the erupting volcano's lava flow. Background design by Tom Dankiewicz. Top right: Mt. Makapu and village. Background design by Tom Dankiewicz. Painting by Hye Jung Kim and Ron Brown.

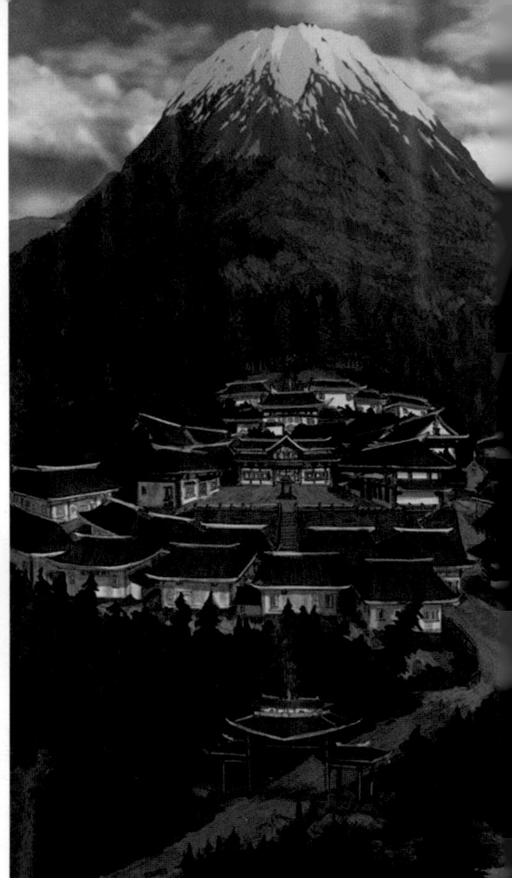

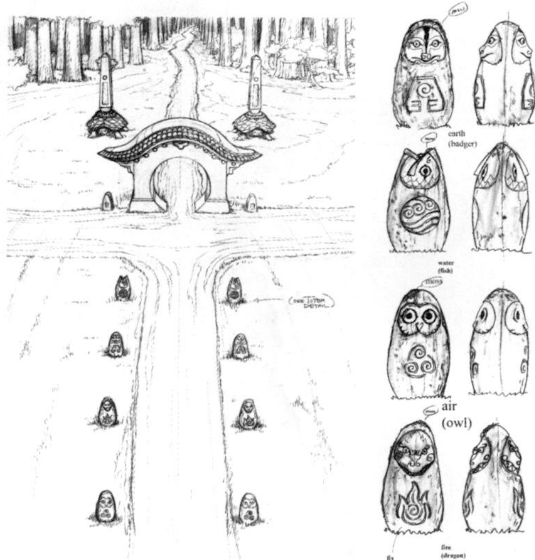

Animal totems line a path leading to Mt. Makapu. The turtle statues were based on statues we saw during our visits to South Korea. Background design by Tom Dankiewicz. Totems by Dave Filoni. Bottom right: Aang and Katara come up with the idea to combine Airbending and Waterbending to move the clouds. Concept by Dave Filoni.

"The Avatar and the Fire Lord" was one of the most complex episodes of the series. It had by far the most background designs of any episode. This ancient version of the throne room was a much more welcoming, light-filled space, as opposed to the dark and imposing place Sozin replaced it with. Wedding courtyard design by Jevon Bue. Fire Lord Sozin's throne room design by Elsa Garagarza. Paintings by Bryan Evans and Hye Jung Kim.

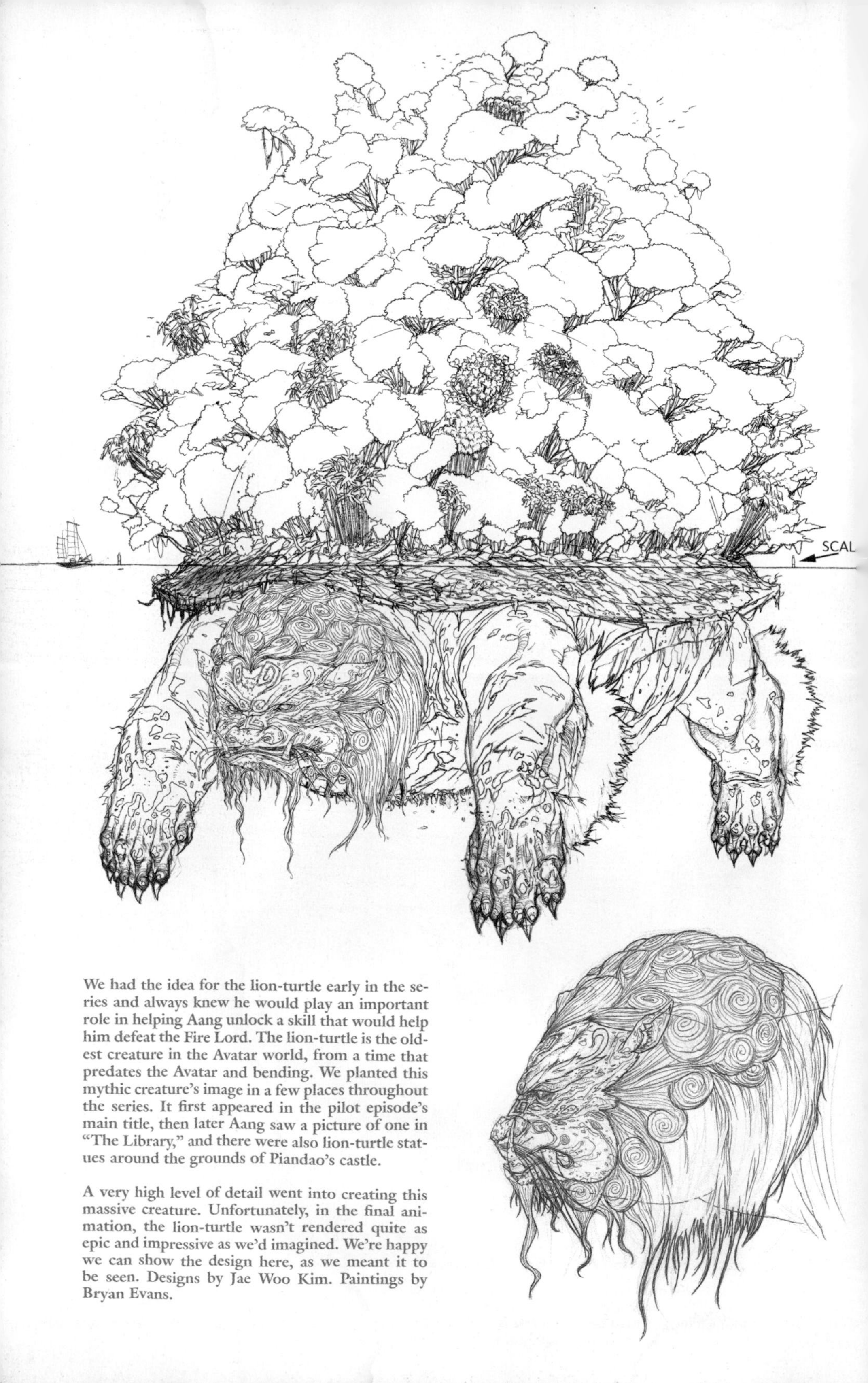

We had the idea for the lion-turtle early in the series and always knew he would play an important role in helping Aang unlock a skill that would help him defeat the Fire Lord. The lion-turtle is the oldest creature in the Avatar world, from a time that predates the Avatar and bending. We planted this mythic creature's image in a few places throughout the series. It first appeared in the pilot episode's main title, then later Aang saw a picture of one in "The Library," and there were also lion-turtle statues around the grounds of Piandao's castle.

A very high level of detail went into creating this massive creature. Unfortunately, in the final animation, the lion-turtle wasn't rendered quite as epic and impressive as we'd imagined. We're happy we can show the design here, as we meant it to be seen. Designs by Jae Woo Kim. Paintings by Bryan Evans.

IF YOU ENJOYED THIS PREVIEW, GET THE FULL-COLOR, 184-PAGE HARDCOVER NOW!

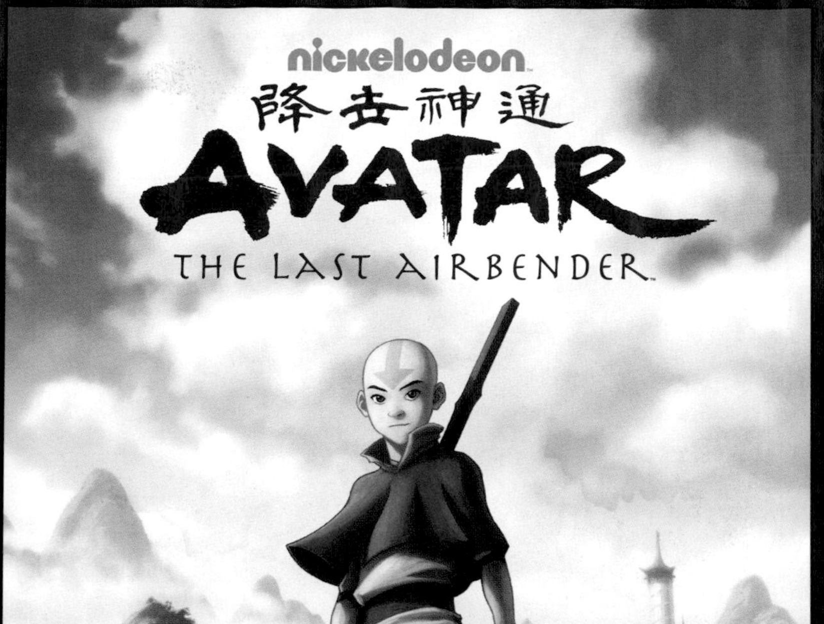

nickelodeon

降世神通

AVATAR

THE LAST AIRBENDER

THE ART OF THE ANIMATED SERIES

Michael Dante DiMartino · *Bryan Konietzko*

Featuring hundreds of exclusive images, including storyboards, character designs, and fight-scene choreography!

AVAILABLE AT YOUR LOCAL
COMICS SHOP OR BOOKSTORE.
To find a comics shop in your area, call 1-888-266-4226
For more information or to order direct, visit
DarkHorse.com or call 1-800-862-0052

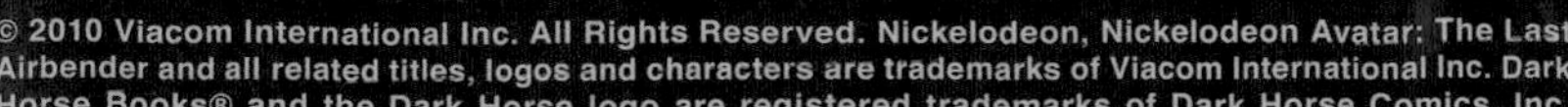

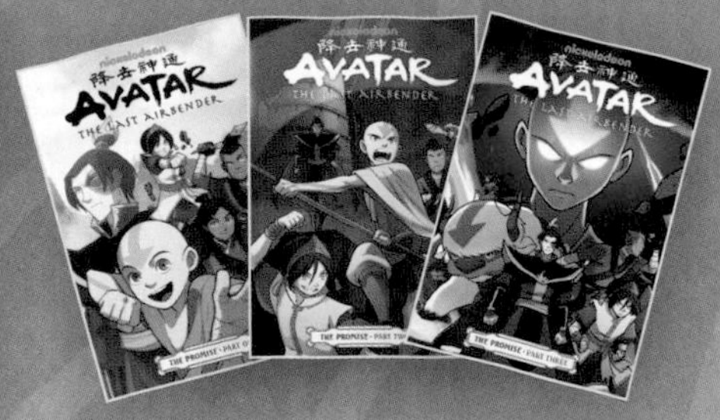

Avatar: The Last Airbender—The Promise Library Edition
978-1-61655-074-5 $39.99

Avatar: The Last Airbender—The Promise Part 1
978-1-59582-811-8 $12.99

Avatar: The Last Airbender—The Promise Part 2
978-1-59582-875-0 $12.99

Avatar: The Last Airbender—The Promise Part 3
978-1-59582-941-2 $12.99

Avatar: The Last Airbender—The Search Library Edition
978-1-61655-226-8 $39.99

Avatar: The Last Airbender—The Search Part 1
978-1-61655-054-7 $12.99

Avatar: The Last Airbender—The Search Part 2
978-1-61655-190-2 $12.99

Avatar: The Last Airbender—The Search Part 3
978-1-61655-184-1 $12.99

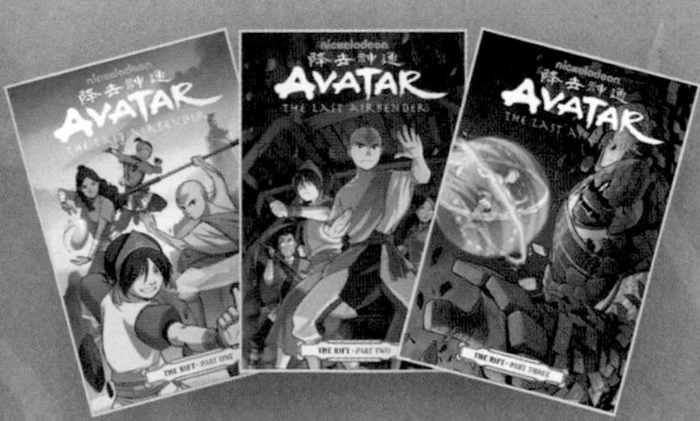

Avatar: The Last Airbender—The Rift Library Edition
978-1-61655-550-4 $39.99

Avatar: The Last Airbender—The Rift Part 1
978-1-61655-295-4 $12.99

Avatar: The Last Airbender—The Rift Part 2
978-1-61655-296-1 $12.99

Avatar: The Last Airbender—The Rift Part 3
978-1-61655-297-8 $10.99

Avatar: The Last Airbender—Smoke and Shadow Library Edition
978-1-50670-013-7 $39.99

Avatar: The Last Airbender—Smoke and Shadow Part 1
978-1-61655-761-4 $12.99

Avatar: The Last Airbender—Smoke and Shadow Part 2
978-1-61655-790-4 $12.99

Avatar: The Last Airbender—Smoke and Shadow Part 3
978-1-61655-838-3 $12.99

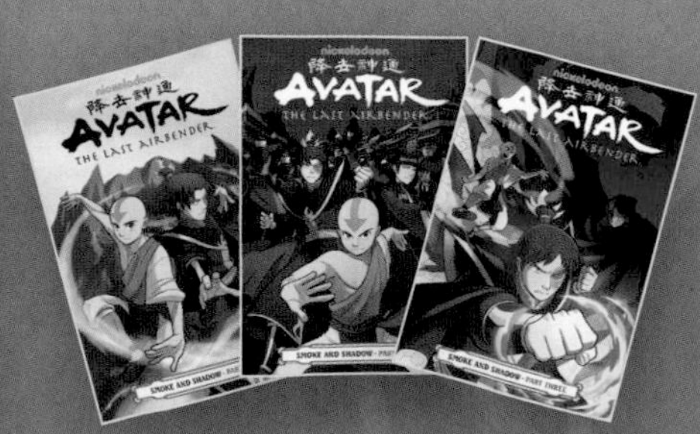